Fat Tire Fun™

The Mountain Biking Trail Guide
for San Luis Obispo County

By Gwen Dawkins and Dirk Franklin

Cover Design by Michael Campbell Design

Book Design by Spyglass Graphics

Illustrations by Joe Blommer

Cover Photos by Dirk Franklin

ISBN 0-9627230-1-0

Printed in the United States of America

Table of Contents

The Rides

San Luis Obispo

Coastal Range

Table of Contents (continued)

Acknowledgments

We'd like to thank...

Our family, friends and fellow mountain bike enthusiasts who encouraged us to write the first edition of *Fat Tire Fun* and demanded we write a second, expanded version.

Joe Blommer for being in the right place, doing the right thing for our cover photo and for contributing some great illustrations; Alan Haag for being our most faithful hammerhead companion and for opening up "Hotel Haag" on our behalf; Francesca Venezia for proofreading a book full of words not found in her dictionary (knobbyhead, techno-weanie, skid lid, etc.); and Bill Charlesworth for not giving up on us and our promises to get this book done.

And of course, we thank our fellow knobbyheads who joined us periodically to help "research" this second edition. To our compadres who rode with us during the making of the first edition of *Fat Tire Fun* but are now too married, too busy, or too out of shape to ride—you know what you're missing—what's up with that?

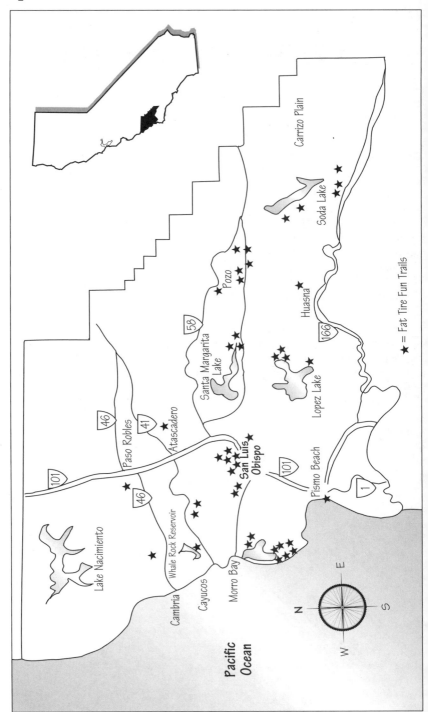

★ = Fat Tire Fun Trails

Getting "Extreme" in SLO

Mountain biking gets a lot of press these days as an "extreme sport." Well, it can be. But you don't have to be heli-dropped from the highest mountain, plow knee-deep through mud, or set new downhilling speed records to love this sport. In fact, you can have an *extremely* great time cruising smooth single track. You can train *extremely* hard on a long, steep climb. And you can feel *extremely* peaceful by getting out on your bike—*and away from everyone and everything*. Yes, mountain biking can be extreme. It can be whatever you want it to be.

And in San Luis Obispo County, the terrain for mountain biking is extremely versatile. From the loose rock on the volcanic peaks, to the hard-packed sand along the coastal range, to the desert-like turf in the south, you'll get experience befitting for the pros. Face it—this is an awesome place to ride! Whether you're a newcomer to the sport or an established hammerhead, you can't beat the riding in SLO County.

Unfortunately, many of the area's popular rides are illegal because they cross private land or designated wilderness areas. Ever since we "cut our teeth" on this sport, we've been in search of great, legal rides throughout the county. And that is how *Fat Tire Fun, The Mountain Biking Trail Guide for San Luis Obispo County* came into being.

Fat Tire Fun is a compilation of 43 of the best, legal rides in San Luis Obispo County. With easy-to-follow trail descriptions and accompanying maps on facing pages, *Fat Tire Fun* is the perfect take-along trail companion. Each ride description includes a complete rating system showing degree of difficulty, total elevation, a full elevation profile, mileage and the all important poison oak factor.

Perhaps most important of all, by following the trails outlined in this book, you'll discover the secret to a committed relationship between you and your bike—*and find it to be extremely satisfying!*

How Rides Are Rated

Each ride description includes a degree of difficulty, elevation gain and profile, mileage and poison oak factor for quick reference. We also list the appropriate topographic maps, which show the area in more detail than the ones contained in this book.

Difficulty

We've rated the difficulty of each ride on a scale from one to five, five being most difficult. This is illustrated by the number of teeth-gritting knobbyheads.

 Level one rides are easy and shorter in length. If you're new to mountain biking or just getting into shape, these are the rides to start with.

 Level two rides are a little more challenging either because of distance, steeper climbs, some technical sections or a combination thereof.

 Level three rides are solid intermediate rides. Appropriately, they fall in the middle of the road when it comes to distance, required technical ability and steeper climbs and descents.

Level four rides require more skill and stamina. These are for people who are serious mountain bikers and/or people seeking a serious workout.

 Reserved for the mountain biking gods. Enough said.

If you are 20 or more pounds overweight, pregnant and in your third trimester, an athletic underachiever, over 90-years-old, under 5-years-old, lame, permanently attached to a remote control or a chronic sufferer of delusions of grandeur, you may not agree with our analyses.

Elevation Gain & Profile

How much climbing a ride requires is important to some people before they're willing to rise to the challenge. The total elevation gain is listed in feet accompanied by the elevation profile, illustrating what you're up against.

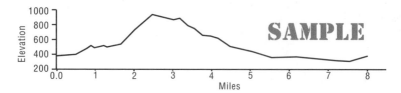

Mileage

Mileage, accompanied by the total elevation gained and elevation profiles are pretty good indicators of what you're getting yourself into. Each ride is also identified as either a Loop or an Out-And-Back. Some ride descriptions also include options for shortcuts, a longer ride or links with other rides.

Note: Your mileage may differ from what appears in this book. As with all things manmade—bike computers aren't perfect. Different equipment, precise calibration and other factors may result in s ight mileage differences.

P.O. Factor

We don't love poison oak, but it loves us. We call it "The Big P.O." and have included handy P.O. Factors for each ride. While poison oak is abundant all over San Luis Obispo County, it's not always obvious. The saying, "Leaves of three, let it be" is a good one; but it's like a l of those grammar rules that apply most of the time but not all of the time. When poison oak loses its leaves, it retains the power to cause you pain. We rate the amount of P.O. in contact with the trail (on a scale from 0-3) ranging from zilch to treacherous jungles of the stuff. So deal with it accordingly. (We always bring soap and water for after-ride-cleanups.)

Topo(s)

The maps contained in this book are very basic. For complete accuracy and detail, we recommend you bring along the appropriate U.S.G.S. topographical map (especially in remote areas).

Getting There

Since the city of San Luis Obispo is central within the county, we provide directions to all trailheads from the city.

The Ride

Each description includes a brief overview of the ride and what to expect.

Maps

The maps included in *Fat Tire Fun* are simple renderings showing the basic route, necessary turns and landmarks. They are not drawn to scale and should not be relied upon for complete accuracy.

☞   This marks the trailhead on each map

⊠   Building

●—●   Gate   - - - - - - - - - -   Dirt Road or Double Track

✗   Picnic Table   ∿∿∿∿   Paved Road

Λ   Campground   ∿∿∿∿∿   Single Track

⚒   Mine   ━━━━━━◁   Creek or Stream

On with the ride . . . .

Mountain Bike Safety

Mountain biking is definitely a sport for thrill seekers. And whether you ride in the big ring or putt around in the small ring, mountain biking can be risky business. Have fun, but don't be reckless. Take precautions to ensure your safety.

- Always wear a helmet!
- Never ride alone.
- Bring plenty of water (2 quarts per person, per day—minimum).
- Bring more food than you think you'll need.
- Carry the necessary tools (see next section).
- Bring extra clothing because weather can change suddenly.
- Have a first aid kit and know how to use it.
- Tuck a safety whistle in you pack in case you need to call for help.

Trailside Repairs

Every cyclist has to make trailside repairs from time to time. Usually it's something simple like a flat tire, but breaking frames, bending forks and losing spokes are not unheard of. This is a bare bones list of tools you should carry.

- Pump
- Patch Kit
- Chain Lube
- Rock (usually accessible on the trail)
- Tire Irons
- Spare Tube
- Small Pliers
- Wrench
- Multitool (or Screw Driver, Allen Wrenches, Chain Tool, and Spoke Wrench)
- Rag (your socks will do in a pinch)

Trail Etiquette

Mountain bikers often share the turf with hikers, equestrians and motorcyclists. Trail courtesies are extremely important, as complaints of reckless riding can and do result in the closure of trails to mountain bikes.

Treat other trail users with respect. Our actions as individual cyclists help shape the opinion of the mountain biking community as a whole. Don't screw it up by bombing by people and horses without warning and without concern.

It's also important to consider the impact mountain biking has on nature. Responsible riding includes careful effort to minimize damage to the natural environment. If ridden with care, mountain bikes fall somewhere in between hikers and horses in terms of their impact on the land. **Tread lightly.**

Trail Dos & Don'ts

- Do stay on existing trails and roads. Blazing new trails encourages others to do the same, which greatly damages plant life and contributes to erosion.

- Do slow down and acknowledge other trail users, especially equestrians as horses may be easily spooked.

- Do allow horses and hikers the right-of-way.

- Do maintain safe speeds.

- Do respect all public and private land.

- Don't leave gates open when they're meant to be shut—don't be the cause of straying livestock.

- Don't litter. If you pack it in, pack it out.

- Don't stop to rest in the middle of a trail. Pull off to the side and out of the way, especially on off-road vehicle trails (ORV).

Trail Maintenance

You enjoy using the trails, so why not help keep them in good condition? There are lots of organized trail maintenance days set up through local cycling clubs and trails committees. And there's no reason why you can't trim a branch here and there while you're riding. In fact, you'll find tools set aside for volunteer trail maintenance on selected trails within Montana De Oro State Park. Pitch in!

Where To Ride

In San Luis Obispo County, mountain bikes are currently allowed on all public paved and dirt roads, jeep trails and Forest Service and State Parks & Recreation system trails (except those within designated wilderness or otherwise restricted areas).

Some portions of the forest are subject to temporary closure because of fire danger or inclement weather. Fire season lasts from July 1 to November 15 each year.

At the time of this printing, all rides in the book were legally open to mountain bikes. However, issues such as erosion, trespassing into restricted areas, fires and other natural disasters may impact the legality of a trail or the condition of a trail. For questions concerning any of these topics contact the appropriate agency. They are all very helpful.

Los Padres National Forest, Santa Lucia Ranger District Office	(805) 925-9538
Arroyo Grande Station	(805) 481-1280
Morro Bay Ranger Station	(805) 528-0513
Pozo Station	(805) 481-1280
State Parks & Recreation, San Luis Obispo Coastal District	(805) 549-3312
Bureau of Land Management (BLM), Caliente Area Office	(805) 861-4236
Goodwin Education Center (for California Valley)	(805) 475-2131

Where Not To Ride

We are fortunate to have such a wide variety of mountain biking opportunities. However, there are a few areas to avoid: private land (without the owner's approval); railroad right-of-way, which includes crossing the tracks; trails posted "No Bikes," and designated wilderness areas.

In San Luis Obispo County, the Los Padres National Forest contains four designated wilderness areas: Garcia, Garcia Mountain, Santa Lucia and Machesna Mountain. Part of the National Wilderness Preservation System, the natural state of these areas is protected by Congress under the Wilderness Act of 1964. No vehicles (including bikes) are permitted. Rangers will issue citations to trespassing cyclists.

Areas posted "No Bikes" include most hiking trails in Morro Bay State Park, parts of Poly Canyon and all trails south of Islay Creek and east of Pecho Valley Road in Montana De Oro State Park. There are also a few trails posted "No Bikes" in various areas within the county.

Quick Reference Lingo Guide

So you have a mountain bike, you know what to do, what not to do, where to ride and which trails may be best for you. But if you're new to the sport, you're probably lacking the proper vocabulary. So, here are some terms to get you talking like a pro.

Billy Goat	A spry rider with a demonstrated skill for climbing.
Blazin'	A controllable high rate of speed.
Bonk	When fatigue and hunger take their toll.
Cairn	A stack of rocks used as a trail marker.
Double Track	Wide dirt paths ranging from dirt roads to the twin tire tracks of rugged jeep trails.
Full Tilt	Pushing maximum performance.
Greenhorn	A novice rider.
Hammer	To give it your physical "all."
Hammerhead	A rider who is virtually unstoppable.
Hammerfest	A weekend or other extended period of time devoted entirely to hard and fast mountain biking.
Involuntary Dismount	Crash
Knobbyhead	One who eats, drinks, sleeps and breathes mountain biking.
Motor Vehicle Stop	A steel barrier to keep motor vehicles out.
Mountainhead	a.k.a. Knobbyhead.
Novice Mark	Chainring grease on a rider's calf.
Single Track	A very narrow trail.
Skid Lid	Helmet
Snake Bite	A flat tire caused by the rim pinching the inner tube and making two matching holes in the tube, a.k.a. pinch flat.
Technical Section	A difficult to treacherous portion of the trail requiring balance, finesse and sometimes courage.
Techno-Weanie	Someone who knows more about bike technology than about riding.
The Big P.O.	Poison Oak, a force to be reckoned with.
Wank	Someone who always says he or she wants to ride, but never actually does.
Water Bar	A log, railroad tie, row of rocks or ruts cut across trail for water runoff purposes.

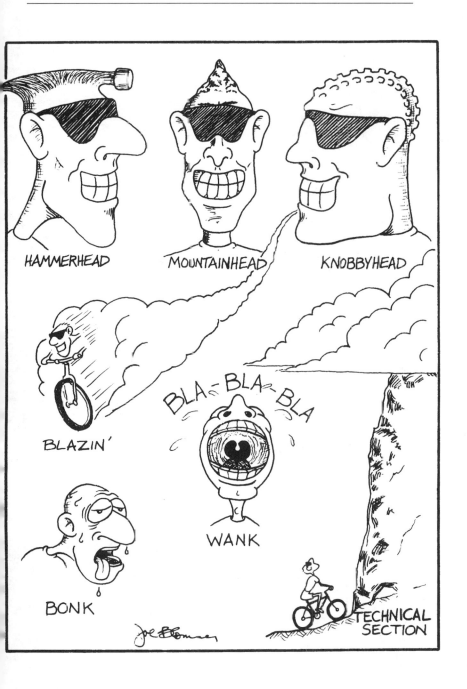

San Luis Obispo

San Luis Obispo Overview

San Luis Obispo's beautiful rolling hills and chaparral-covered mountains provide a wealth of mountain biking opportunities right around town. The rides range from a "quickie" in Poly Canyon to the 38-mile loop across West Cuesta Ridge. If you live in town, you should be able to get to any of the trails contained in this section in less than 15 minutes.

Of course, one of the best attributes of the area is the weather. The temperatures in and around San Luis Obispo are consistently mild. While there are short periods of rain and heat from time to time, you can't beat the weather for year-round fat tire fun!

Some trails are located in Poly Canyon on the Cal Poly campus. Because of the many agricultural programs offered at Cal Poly, livestock often roams freely in some of the areas we have outlined for riding. Likewise, a strong horticultural focus means certain areas of the land are reserved for sensitive plant life and therefore, off limits to bikes.

In the past, Poly Canyon has been closed to bikes because some riders repeatedly chose to disregard restricted areas and interfered with livestock. Now that it's open to bikes again, DON'T SCREW IT UP!

When riding in Poly Canyon, keep these basic rules in mind:

1. Always leave gates as you found them (there are lots of gates).
2. Don't chase livestock.
3. Leave your dog at home (they are not allowed in Poly Canyon).
4. Stay on established trails.
5. If a sign says "Keep Out" or "No Bikes" stay out.

While riding in Poly Canyon, you may notice other trail users traveling between the campus property and West Cuesta Ridge (or vice versa). Both of these areas are open to bikes, but users must cross railroad tracks to pass from one area to the next. However, the Southern Pacific Railroad does not grant the right to cross the tracks, making this an illegal maneuver. Therefore, directions to connect trails in these two areas are not included in this book.

San Luis Obispo Overview

Poly Canyon Loop

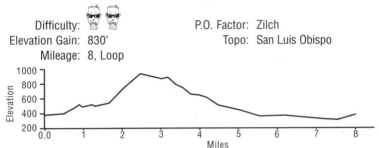

Difficulty: 😎 😎   P.O. Factor: Zilch
Elevation Gain: 830'   Topo: San Luis Obispo
Mileage: 8, Loop

This is a great beginner and intermediate ride, providing peaceful surroundings in a central location. If you live on campus, you can't beat it for quick fun.

Getting There

From US 101 take the Cal Poly exit and head toward campus. Turn right on Perimeter Road. Around the bend, turn right on Poly Canyon Road. A gate marks the entrance to Poly Canyon. If you drive to the trailhead, you will need a parking permit available from dispensers in the lots.

The Ride

Starting at the steel gate, pedal up the dirt road that parallels Brizziolari Creek. You will soon pass a stone arch on the left, which marks the entrance to the experimental architectural site. Pass the farm house and barn, going through the first in a series of gates. At 1.7 miles you will pass through the fourth gate near a small corral. The road begins climbing here.

After about a mile of climbing, you will reach the top of the hill at 2.5 miles. Tough & Dirty Slide (turn page for details) cuts left. However, go through the gate and begin your descent. Just past a small stream, the road intersects as a "T." Going right heads to the railroad tracks. But go left, heading downhill. At 3.4 miles, veer right as the road forks. You will come to Stenner Ranch at 3.8 miles. Pass through the gate, cross the wooden bridge, then turn left.

Continue on as the road turns to pavement at 5.6 miles under the train trestle. Turn left on Mt. Bishop Road, then left again just past the Poultry Unit. At 7.2 miles turn left onto the dirt shoulder at Highland Road. Bear left, going uphill just beyond the train bridge. At 7.6 miles, turn right on to Via Carta Road. At the stop sign, turn left onto Feedmill Road. Bear right, going uphill on the dirt road. Turn right on Poly Canyon Road, returning to the trailhead, 8 miles.

Poly Canyon Loop

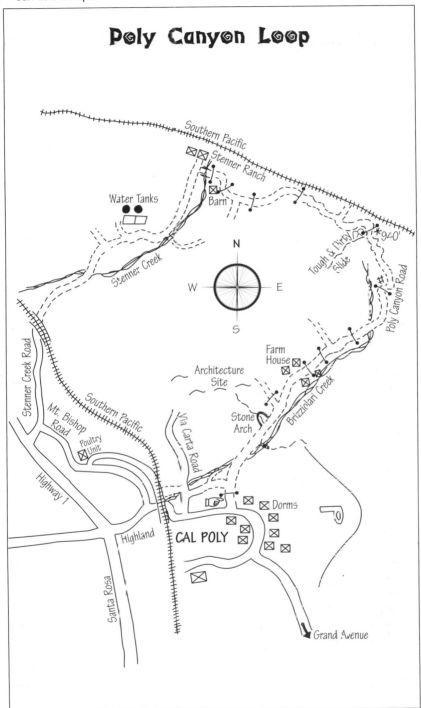

T☺ugh & Dirty Slide

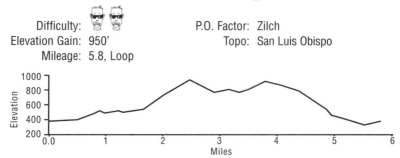

Difficulty: 😎 😎   P.O. Factor: Zilch
Elevation Gain: 950'   Topo: San Luis Obispo
Mileage: 5.8, Loop

This ride through beautiful Poly Canyon starts out with a long climb on a graded dirt road, but then transforms to a fun single track across oak-studded ridges.

Getting There
From US 101 take the Cal Poly exit and head toward campus. Turn right on Perimeter Road. Around the bend, turn right on Poly Canyon Road. A gate marks the entrance to Poly Canyon. If you drive to the trailhead, you will need a parking permit available from dispensers in the lots.

The Ride
Starting at the steel gate, pedal up the dirt road that parallels Brizziolari Creek. You will pass a stone arch on the left before arriving at a farm house and barn. Bypass the first of several gates. At 1.7 miles you will pass through the fourth gate near a small corral. The road begins climbing here.

After about a mile of climbing, you will reach the top of the hill at 2.5 miles. Take the unmarked "Tough & Dirty Slide" single track as it cuts left. Pass through a rocky outcropping and bear left across the ridge. You will pass through a barb wire gate, followed shortly by a steel gate. At 3.3 miles you will come out at a dirt road. Take it right, uphill (going left takes you back down to Poly Canyon Road). Just ahead, pass through another gate. Continue uphill. At the top of the climb, turn left at the fence line onto a double track. Four miles into the ride pass through another gate and follow the trail downhill. Just ahead, turn right onto a faint single track which soon becomes a well established trail. At the saddle, take a jeep road right. The architectural site is down below on the left. Uphill on the left is a lookout point.

At 4.4 miles, pass through a gate and continue on toward the saddle. Bear right, onto the double track that drops into Horse Canyon. Just past the small reservoir, enter a large corral. Ride through this area slowly, as the horses are loose and can be easily spooked. Close the gates at both ends! Continue on, keeping to the left of the horse arena and stalls. Pavement begins at Via Carta Road, which is a long, straight downhill. At the stop sign, turn left onto Feedmill Road. Bear right, uphill onto a dirt road. Turn right on Poly Canyon Road, returning to the trailhead, 5.8 miles.

Tough & Dirty Slide

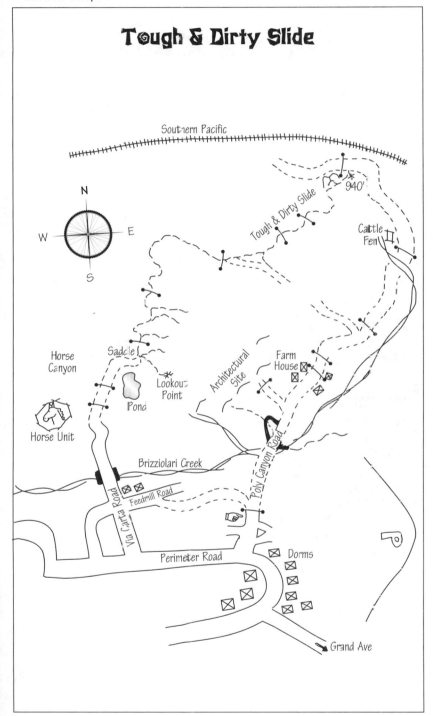

Prefumo Canyon

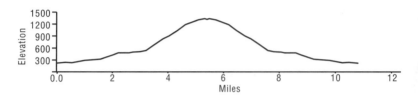

Difficulty: 😎 😎   P.O. Factor: Zilch
Elevation Gain: 1280'   Topos: San Luis Obispo,
Mileage: 10.8, Out-And-Back   Morro Bay South

This scenic dirt and paved road winds its way along creek beds, ancient oaks, quaint ranches and rolling hills. Spectacular views await you at the top!

Getting There

Prefumo Canyon Road intersects Los Osos Valley Road between Madonna Road and Foothill in San Luis Obispo. Turn onto Prefumo Canyon Road. Park at the dirt turnout just ahead on the left side.

The Ride

Start pedaling up Prefumo Canyon Road which soon narrows. At 2.6 miles the road turns to dirt at a cattle guard. At 3.2 miles the road begins to steepen. At 4.4 miles the road returns to pavement and continues climbing.

Pavement ends again at 4.6 miles near a rocky outcropping on the right. For an outstanding view, leave your bike on the roadside and climb up to the large rock. The elevation here is 1174'. From this vantage point you can see six of the "Seven Sisters." These volcanic peaks form a line from San Luis Obispo to Morro Rock.

Pedal on to the top of the range. You'll come to a ranch and lots of eucalyptus trees at 5.4 miles. Turn around here and head back the way you came for a fast downhill*. You will get back to the car at 10.8 miles.

*For a longer ride, turn the page for the Diehard Version.

Prefumo Canyon

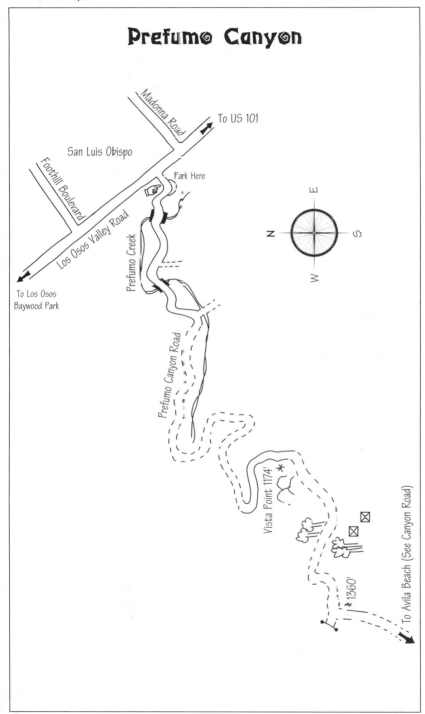

Prefumo Canyon
DIEHARD VERSION

Difficulty: 😎 😎 😎   P.O. Factor: Zilch
Elevation Gain: 1630'   Topos: San Luis Obispo, Pismo
Mileage: 19.6, Loop   Beach, Morro Bay South
                                           Port San Luis

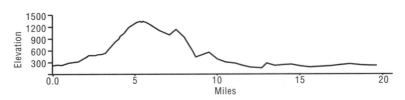

This back country road winds past quaint ranches and rolling hills. Great views, a steady climb, fast downhills and distance—who could ask for more?

Getting There
Prefumo Canyon Road intersects Los Osos Valley Road between Madonna Road and Foothill in San Luis Obispo. Turn onto Prefumo Canyon Road. Park at the dirt turnout just ahead on the left side.

The Ride
Start pedaling on Prefumo Canyon Road which soon narrows. At 2.64 miles the road turns to dirt at a cattle guard. At 3.21 miles the road begins to steepen. At 4.4 miles the road returns to pavement and continues climbing.

Pavement ends again at 4.6 miles near a rocky outcropping on the right. For an outstanding view, leave your bike on the roadside and climb up to the large rock. The elevation here is 1174'. From this vantage point you can see six of the "Seven Sisters." These volcanic peaks form a line from San Luis Obispo to Morro Rock.

Pedal on to the top of the range. You'll come to a ranch and lots of eucalyptus trees at 5.4 miles. Just around the next curve the road becomes See Canyon Road. Keep winding your way down past homes and ranches until reaching San Luis Bay Road at 13.5 miles. Turn left on San Luis Bay Road (Turning right will take you to Avila Beach). Then turn left on Ontario Road at 15.6 miles. At the intersection with Higuera, veer left going under the freeway. Follow the road as it parallels the freeway. You will pass a cool octagonal-shaped barn on the right at 16.9 miles. Take a left on Los Osos Valley Road at 17.3 miles, crossing over the freeway. You will cross Madonna Road at 18.7 miles. At 19.3 miles, turn left on Prefumo Canyon Road, reaching your car at 19.6 miles.

Prefumo Canyon
DIEHARD VERSION

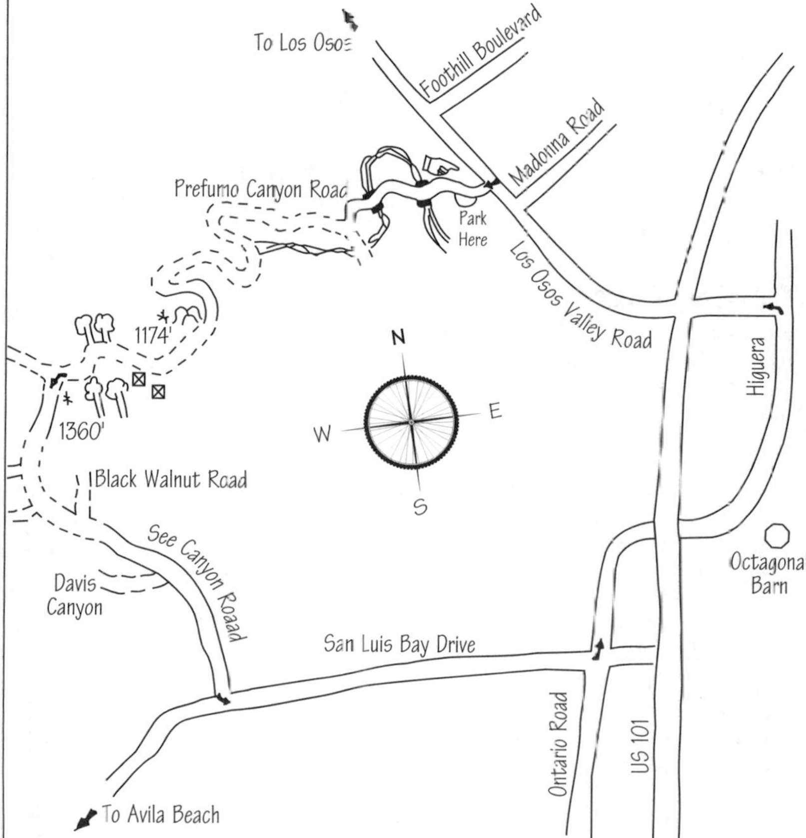

To Los Osos

Foothill Boulevard

Madonna Road

Prefumo Canyon Road

Park Here

Los Osos Valley Road

1174'

1360'

N
W — E
S

Black Walnut Road

Higuera

See Canyon Road

Davis Canyon

Octagonal Barn

San Luis Bay Drive

Ontario Road

US 101

To Avila Beach

East Cuesta Ridge

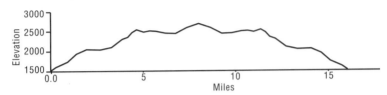

Difficulty: 👤 👤 👤   P.O. Factor: Zilch
Elevation Gain: 1650'   Topos: San Luis Obispo,
Mileage: 16, Out-And-Back   Lopez Mountain

This ride offers great views of San Luis Obispo and its surrounding areas. As it follows graded Mt. Lowe Road, this ride provides moderate, yet sustained climbing and little need for technical expertise.

Getting There

From US 101 in San Luis Obispo, head north climbing Cuesta grade. Just after passing the summit, turn right near a pay phone. It doubles back into a parking area. Park here, but don't block the gate.

The Ride

Climb over the locked gate and start climbing Mt. Lowe Road. After about a mile of climbing, the road levels out before coming to a cattle guard at 1.4 miles. A second cattle guard is at 1.9 miles. For the next two miles, take in the great views of the San Luis Basin from Morro Rock to Pismo Beach as you continue climbing.

At 4.2 miles you will pass a road to the left and a firebreak to the right. Keep going straight. Just ahead you will see a radio tower and the road to it cutting left. Continue uphill to the right. You'll reach an area with great vistas at 4.6 miles. On the left, at about 5.3 miles, is the entrance to the Santa Lucia Wilderness Area and the Upper Lopez Canyon trailhead. That trail is off limits to bikes. Keep going uphill to the right. Just ahead, bear left at the "Y."

At about 6.8 miles you'll start another climb. Keep climbing until you reach a gate to private property at 8.0 miles. Turn around here. You'll pass the entrance to the Wilderness Area trailhead at just past 10.6 miles and the two cattle guards at 14.1 and 14.6 miles. You'll be back at the start of the ride at 16 miles.

East Cuesta Ridge

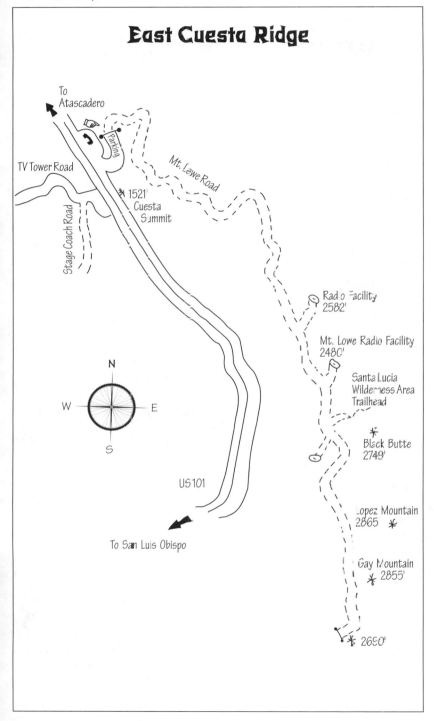

To Atascadero

Parking

Mt. Lewe Road

TV Tower Road

Stage Coach Road

* 1521'
Cuesta Summit

Radio Facility
2582'

Mt. Lowe Radio Facility
2480'

Santa Lucia
Wilderness Area
Trailhead

* Black Butte
2749'

N

W — E

S

US 101

Lopez Mountain
2865 *

Gay Mountain
* 2855'

To San Luis Obispo

* 2690'

West Cuesta Ridge

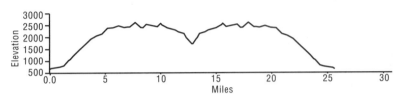

Difficulty: 🕶🕶🕶🕶   P.O. Factor: Zilch
Elevation Gain: 3850   Topos: San Luis Obispo,
Mileage: 25.6, Out-And-Back   Atascadero

This is pure training ride with plenty of climbing on paved and dirt roads. The rewards for your work are great views and exhilarating downhills!

Getting There

From US 101 in San Luis Obispo, head north. Just after passing town and the Monterey Street exit, turn left onto Stage Coach Road. Park in the dirt on the right side.

The Ride

Start pedaling up Stage Coach Road as it steadily climbs and winds its way to the top of Cuesta Grade. You'll reach the paved TV Tower Road at 2.7 miles. (There is alternative parking here if you want a shorter ride.) Turn left and continue climbing.

Stay on the paved road ignoring a few dirt roads that join from both sides. You will enter the Botanical Area after 3 miles of climbing. This is one of only three places in the world where the Sargant Cypress grows. Keep following the road, leaving the Botanical Area at 7.7 miles. From here the road has several steep climbs and descents. You'll pass a gate down to the left posted "No Motor Vehicles" at 8.4 miles.

At 10 miles, the road to Tassajera Peak splits to the right. Continue straight, passing a gate and a sign marked "No Target Shooting." The road, now dirt, begins descending. Veer left as the Cerro Alto Jeep Trail joins from behind a large embankment and steel gate at 12.3 miles. Just ahead, keep going straight as the AT&T cable route joins from the right.

You will enter a eucalyptus grove at 12.7 miles. Just ahead you'll come to a large dirt mound as the trail narrows. Turn around here and head back the way you came. (Diehards can continue on through Cerro Alto and onto Highway 1. See the next page.)

You'll arrive back at the start of pavement at 15.6 miles. You'll enter the Botanical Area at 17.9 and leave it at 19.9 miles. After a long, fast descent, you'll be back at the intersection with Stage Coach Road at 22.9 miles. Turn right, heading downhill and return to your car at 25.6 miles.

West Cuesta Ridge

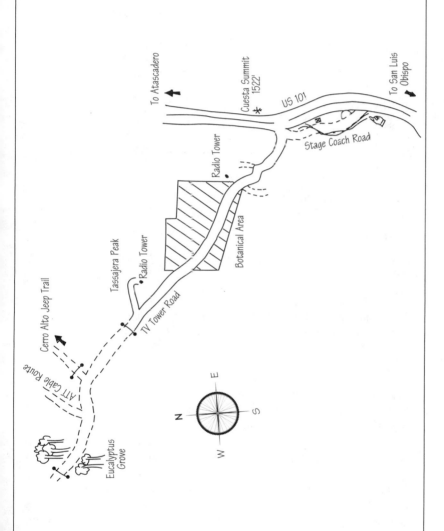

West Cuesta Ridge
DIEHARD VERSION

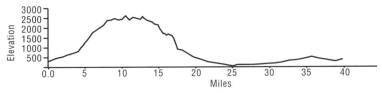

Difficulty: [icons]   P.O. Factor: [icons]

Elevation Gain: 4570'   Topos: San Luis Obispo, Atascadero,
Mileage: 39.8, Loop   Morro Bay North,
                                      Morro Bay South

This is great ride for the advanced rider. It starts with a long warm-up, then lots of steady climbing, then some fun single track and finally, a mostly flat return trip.

Getting There

From US 101 in San Luis Obispo, head north and exit at Monterey Street. Park near the northbound onramp.

The Ride

From Monterey Street, start pedaling up the onramp onto US 101. At 2.7 miles, cross the freeway and turn onto Stage Coach Road. The road soon turns to dirt. You'll pass a farm house a mile up the road. After crossing over San Luis Creek the road begins to climb.

At the junction with TV Tower Road at 5.5 miles, turn left, uphill on pavement. Continue climbing this main road as other roads split to both sides. You'll enter the Cuesta Botanical Area at 8.5 miles. You will leave the Botanical Area at about 10.5 miles. From here the road has several steep climbs and descents.

At 12.8 miles, the road to Tassajera Peak splits to the right. But continue straight, passing a gate. The road, now dirt, begins descending. At 15.1 miles, the Cerro Alto Jeep Trail joins on the right from behind a large embankment and steel gate. Continue going straight, passing the AT&T Cable Route on the right at 15.2 miles.

Keep left as you enter a eucalyptus grove at 15.6 miles. The trail soon narrows and crosses a mound then a steel pipe fence. Bypass and continue. At 16 miles, take a hard right switchback at the intersection and climb uphill.

At the junction at 16.8 miles, bear right, going downhill on the single track. After a fun descent, you will cross a creek at 17.4 miles. Just ahead, bear right (a faint trail goes left). You'll cross another creek and come out on the paved road within Cerro Alto Campground. Turn left, heading to Highway 41.

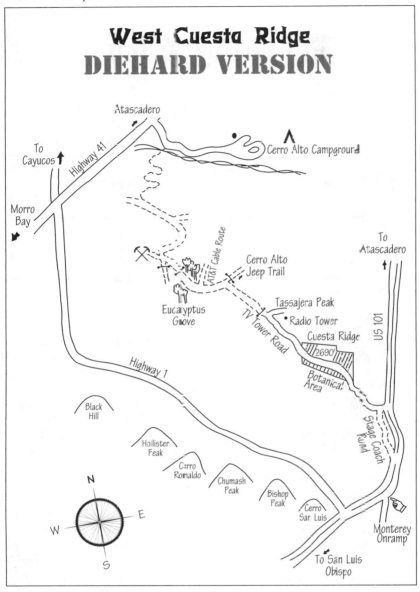

West Cuesta Ridge
DIEHARD VERSION

Turn left on Highway 41 and follow its curves downhill to Highway 1 South. At 25.1 miles, turn left onto Highway 1. Now on your way back to San Luis Obispo, you will pass Cuesta College at 32.7 miles and then Camp San Luis.

At 37.7 miles, cross Foothill Boulevard and continue through town until coming to Monterey Street. Turn left, returning to your car at 39.8 miles.

Morning Glory

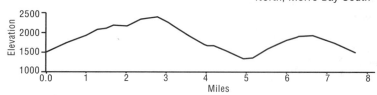

Difficulty: 👓👓👓   P.O. Factor: 🍂
Elevation Gain: 1590'   Topos: San Luis Obispo,
Mileage: 7.7, Loop   Atascadero, Morro Bay
                                                 North, Morro Bay South

This ride has a little of everything: road, single track and double track. But don't let the road fool you, this ride's not just a road grind. The single track section requires plenty of finesse and rewards with lots of fun.

Getting There

From US 101 in San Luis Obispo, head north up Cuesta Grade. At the summit, turn left into the parking area near a pay phone.

The Ride

Start pedaling up TV Tower Road. Just after the one-mile-mark you'll pass a jeep road known as Shooters. Stay on the paved road as it steadily climbs. At 2.5 miles you'll pass a road that splits right, heading to the TV towers. At 2.8 miles take the jeep trail, called Morning Glory, on the left just before the sign for the Cuesta Ridge Botanical Area. Heading downhill, the trail narrows and takes several sweeping turns before arriving at an unmarked single track cutting abruptly left at 3.6 miles. Take it. At 4 miles make a sharp left turn at the fork.

The trail soon makes a series of switchbacks and crosses a creek bottom at 5 miles. After cutting through a small gully, the single track meets double track at 5.2 miles. This is Shooters, the fire road you passed earlier. Take it uphill to the left. (Private property is on the right.) Keep climbing Shooters, passing two gates at 5.5 and 6 miles respectively. At 6.3 miles you will come to an intersection with Roller Coasters Road. Turn left, passing another gate and reaching TV Tower Road at 6.7 miles. Turn right for a fast downhill, returning to your car, 7.7 miles.

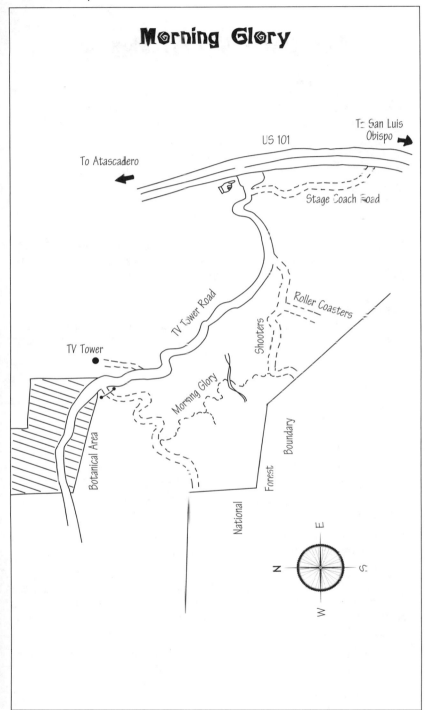

Morning Glory

Roller Coasters

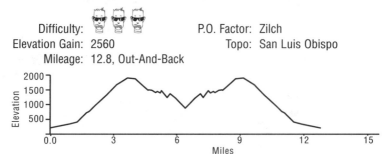

Difficulty: 👹👹👹   P.O. Factor: Zilch
Elevation Gain: 2560   Topo: San Luis Obispo
Mileage: 12.8, Out-And-Back

On your way through Cuesta Grade by car, you have a perfect view of Roller Coasters to the west. Long, steep, rolling ups and downs are what this ride is all about. This ride will test your climbing ability.

Getting There

From San Luis Obispo head north on US 101. About 2.7 miles after passing the Monterey Street exit, turn left onto Stage Coach Road. Park in the dirt pullout near the trees on the right.

The Ride

Pedal up Stage Coach Road, passing a farm house just ahead. The climbing starts at about 1.3 miles. A few roads cut in along the way, but stay on Stage Coach Road until reaching the junction with TV Tower Road at 2.7 miles. Turn left on the paved road and climb.

At 3.7 miles take the dirt road that cuts left, bypassing the gate. This is known as "Shooters." At 4.0 miles, you'll come to a fork. Shooters continues right around the corner. But go left on the double track next to a partial fence (a single track goes uphill at the far left).

Pass through a gate at 4.6 miles. Just ahead, take the single track right at the fork. Keep climbing and descending along the rolling hills. You'll pass through another gate at 5.6 miles. Continue straight uphill.

The road makes a sharp U-turn at 6.0 miles. Soon you'll ride through a narrow washed out section of the trail. You'll reach a junction at 6.4 miles. The railroad tracks are to the right and a single track goes left. Turnaround here and head back the way you came (Southern Pacific Railroad does not grant a right to cross the tracks).

Ride the ups and downs until arriving back at the junction with Shooters. Take Shooters uphill to the right. You'll reach TV Tower Road at 9.1 miles. Turn right heading downhill. At 10.1 miles, take Stage Coach Road right, returning to your car at 12.8 miles.

Roller Coasters

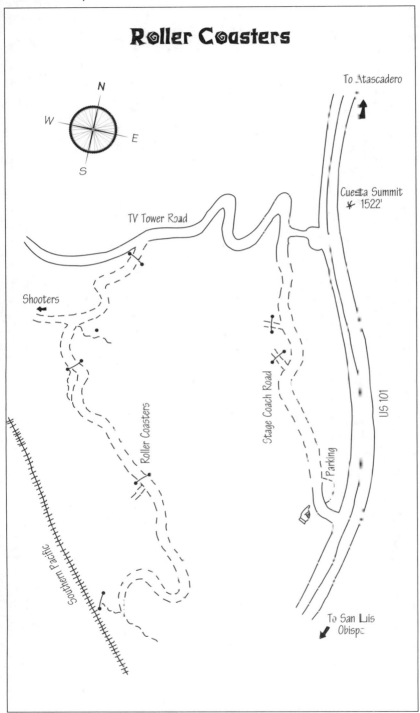

Coastal Range

Coastal Range Overview

Anchored by Morro Bay to the north and Pismo Beach to the south, the Coastal Range offers some of the most beautiful trails in San Luis Obispo County. With a view of the ocean from every trail, many rides also include spectacular views of Morro Rock.

First noted in the respective journals of Miguel Costanso and Father Juan Crespi during the Portola Expedition of 1769, Morro Rock was described as a crown-shaped rock, or "morro." The name stuck and the rock has become an well recognized landmark along the Central Coast. Today, this 578' volcanic "plug" is a registered California Historical Landmark. As a mountain biker, you can look forward to views of the Rock few others will ever see.

Trails near Morro Bay include the Cabrillo Area of Morro Bay State Park and the 8,000-acre Montana De Oro State Park. Both of these areas are former ranch lands, long prized for their rugged beauty. Today, they provide a vast network of trails for everyone to enjoy.

Not far from Morro Bay is Cerro Alto. This mountain peak, tucked between Morro Bay and Atascadero, is another great place to climb for exhilarating views. And remember, what goes up must come down!

To the south is Pismo Beach. Not exactly your typical mountain biking experience, riding along the hard-packed sand at the water's edge will give your legs a great workout. However, mechanically speaking, it's not a good idea to ride in the water.

Temperatures along the Coastal Range are typically cooler than San Luis Obispo and much cooler than the northern and southern areas of the county. Come on out to beat the heat and enjoy the ride!

Coastal Range Overview

Islay Creek Trail

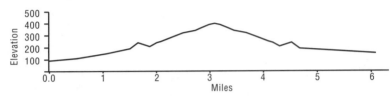

Difficulty: 😎 P.O. Factor: Zilch
Elevation Gain: 400' Topo: Morro Bay South
Mileage: 6.2, Out-And-Back

This graded dirt road at the coast is a great starting point for the greenhorn rider or anyone looking for a leisurely, scenic ride.

Getting There

From San Luis Obispo or Highway 101, take Los Osos Valley Road through the town of Los Osos. Continuing on, the road becomes Pecho Valley Road. The trailhead is approximately 2.5 miles past the Montana De Oro State Park entrance sign. Park on the right just beyond the Islay Creek Trailhead.

The Ride

Bypass the steel gate and follow this easygoing dirt road as it parallels Islay Creek. At 1.1 miles Reservoir Flats Trail cuts in from the right. Keep going straight. Cross a small wooden bridge at 1.9 miles. You will pass South Fork Islay Trail on the right at 2.1 miles then Barranca Trail on the left.

You'll come to another small bridge at 2.8 miles. Just ahead is an old barn. Pedaling another 0.2 miles brings you to the trailhead for East Boundary Trail. However, continue straight ahead on Islay Creek Trail until it ends at the park boundary and a locked gate at 3.1 miles. Turn around here and return to Pecho Valley Road and the trailhead, 6.2 miles.

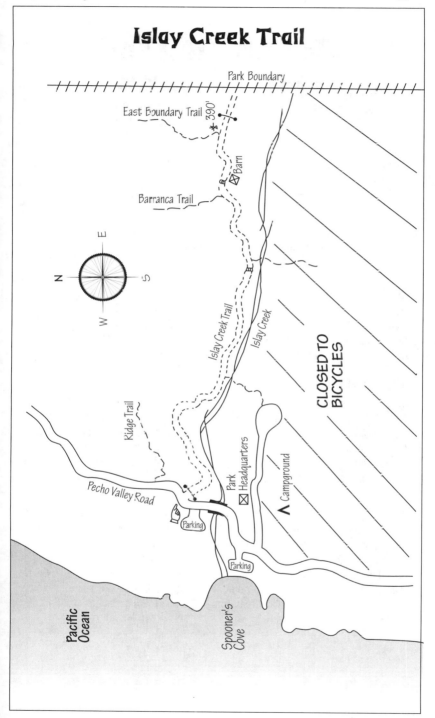

Islay Creek Trail

Park Boundary

East Boundary Trail

390'

Barn

Barranca Trail

Islay Creek Trail

Islay Creek

CLOSED TO BICYCLES

Ridge Trail

Pecho Valley Road

Park Headquarters

Campground

Parking

Parking

Pacific Ocean

Spooner's Cove

Barranca Trail

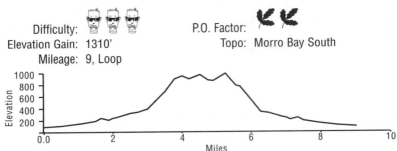

Difficulty: 😎 😎 😎   P.O. Factor: 🍂 🍂
Elevation Gain: 1310'   Topo: Morro Bay South
Mileage: 9, Loop

Barranca Trail is one of the newest trails in Montana De Oro State Park. This fun loop offers plenty of challenging climbs and tight, twisty single track descents.

Getting There

From San Luis Obispo or Highway 101, take Los Osos Valley Road through the town of Los Osos. Continuing on, the road becomes Pecho Valley Road. The trailhead is approximately 2.5 miles past the Montana De Oro State Park entrance sign. Park on the right just beyond the Islay Creek trailhead.

The Ride

Bypass the gate at Islay Creek Trail and pedal along this easygoing dirt road. At 1.1 miles, Reservoir Flats trail cuts in from the right. Keep going straight, crossing a small bridge at 1.9 miles. At 2.9 miles you will cross another wooden bridge. An abandoned barn is ahead on the right. At 3.0 miles take East Boundary Trail to the left, climbing uphill. After a long, technical climb you'll arrive at a grassy summit at 3.8 miles. (Take a few minutes to improve the trail with the tools stored here for volunteer trail maintenance.)

Back on your bike, you'll cross a bridge at 4.2 miles and begin a series of small climbs and descents. Just after a short, steep climb, take the unmarked trail to the left at 4.9 miles. Now on Barranca Trail, you'll reach a fork at 5.3 miles. To take a break, there's a picnic table uphill to the left. Otherwise, turn right heading downhill. Soon you will encounter a series of fun switchbacks. At 5.7 miles there's another tool stand. Keep going and soon you'll descend back onto Islay Creek Trail. Turn right on Islay Creek Trail at 6.3 miles and pedal back to the trailhead, 9 miles.

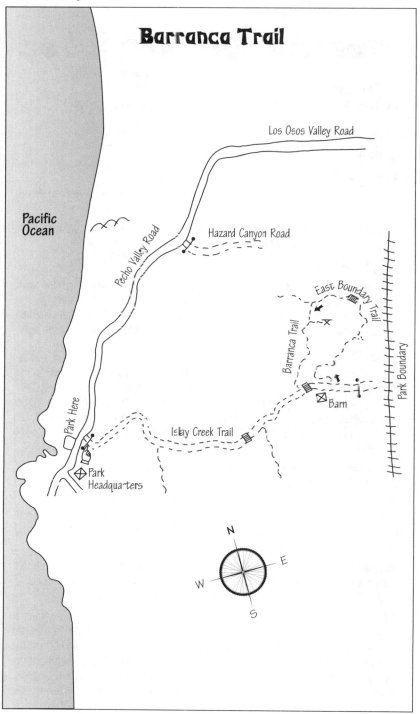

Barranca Trail

Los Osos Valley Road

Pacific
Ocean

Pecho Valley Road

Hazard Canyon Road

East Boundary Trail

Barranca Trail

Park Boundary

Barn

Park Here

Islay Creek Trail

Park
Headquarters

N
E
W
S

Montana De Oro Loop

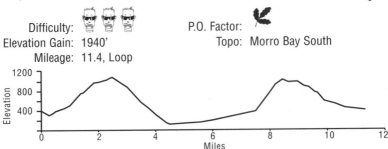

Difficulty: 👓👓👓   P.O. Factor: 🍂
Elevation Gain: 1940'   Topo: Morro Bay South
Mileage: 11.4, Loop

Mostly single track, the ride is both physically and technically challenging. Plus it's gorgeous and packed with fun. This is epic Montana De Oro riding.

Getting There

From San Luis Obispo or Highway 101, take Los Osos Valley Road through the town of Los Osos. Continuing on, the road becomes Pecho Valley Road. Pass the Montana De Oro entrance sign. Just over the crest of the hill, on the left, is a gate marked "Group Horse Camp." Park near the gate or in the dirt pullout just past it on the right.

The Ride

Starting at the gate, pedal up Hazard Canyon Road, passing the Horse Camp on the right. Bypass the steel gate and continue on to Manzanita Trail at 0.8 miles. Take Manzanita Trail. It starts out as a fun single track then begins a long, steady climb over a series of water bars. At 1.4 miles, it intersects with East Boundary Trail. Go right. Just ahead the trail splits. Go left, heading uphill. Take an immediate right onto Ridge Trail (East Boundary Trail climbs to the left).

After some technical climbing over loose shale, you will reach a summit at 1.8 miles. The elevation here is about 990'. Turn left, continuing on Ridge Trail. A second climb begins at 2.3 miles. You will reach Hazard Peak at 2.5 miles, elevation 1076'.

The trail now descends, crossing an old fence line. After a rough downhill, the trail levels out at a sandy section at 3.7 miles. At 4.4 miles, turn left onto Pecho Valley Road, then left again onto Islay Creek Trail at 4.5 miles.

Bypass the steel gate and continue several miles on this graded dirt road. You will pass a barn at 7.2 miles. Just past a 2-mile marker, turn left onto East Boundary Trail at 7.5 miles. This climb is almost a mile long and fairly technical.

After a short descent, you'll cross a wooden bridge at 8.6 miles. Next comes a series of short climbs and descents. At 9.4 miles Barranca Trail forks to the left. Keep going straight. At 9.6 miles take Ridge Trail to the right. Just ahead at the fork, take Manzanita Trail to the right. At 9.7 miles the trail forks left, but keep right on East Boundary Trail. The trail soon descends over lots of water bars as it parallels the park boundary fence. After a creek crossing at 9.9 miles, the trail bends left. Pass Manzanita Trail at 10.6 miles and return to the trailhead at 11.4 miles.

Montana De Oro Loop

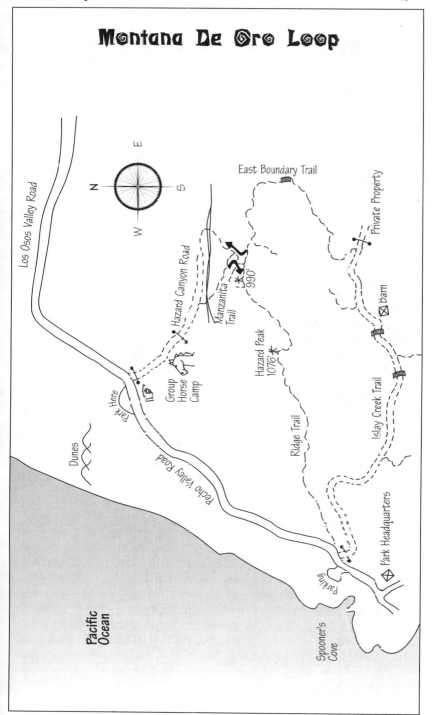

Los Osos Valley Road

East Boundary Trail

Private Property

Hazard Canyon Road

Manzanita Trail

990

⊠ barn

Hazard Peak
1076'

Group
Horse
Camp

Islay Creek Trail

Park Here

Ridge Trail

Dunes

Pecho Valley Road

Park Headquarters

Parking

Pacific
Ocean

Spooner's
Cove

Bloody Nose Trail

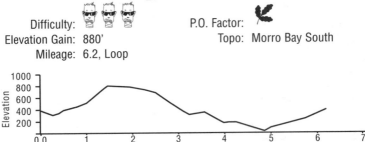

Difficulty: 😎 😎 😎   P.O. Factor: 🍂
Elevation Gain: 880'   Topo: Morro Bay South
Mileage: 6.2, Loop

This trail rocks! Loose shale, rocks and ruts make it challenging and sand makes it hard work in spots—but it's all worth it. Get ready to be rewarded for your efforts!

Getting There

From San Luis Obispo or Highway 101, take Los Osos Valley Road through the town of Los Osos. Continuing on, the road becomes Pecho Valley Road. Pass the Montana De Oro entrance sign. Just over the crest of the hill, on the left, is a gate marked "Group Horse Camp." Park near the gate or in the dirt pullout just past it on the right.

The Ride

Bypass the steel gate and pedal down Hazard Canyon Road passing the horse camp on the right. Pass a second gate at 0.4 miles and go uphill. At 0.8 miles take Manzanita Trail to the right. Starting out as a single track winding along a creek bottom, the trail soon starts a long, steady climb uphill over a series of water bars. At 1.4 miles, turn right as the trail intersects with East Boundary. Just ahead you will come to a junction—keep going straight on Manzanita Trail.

From here, follow the single track along a ridge offering great views of the ocean and the Horse Camp down below. At 1.9 miles a spur trail goes off to the right. Stay left however and descend as the trail gets wider and rocky. Ahead, the trail gets sandy, real sandy, as it cuts through a head-high ravine. You'll come out at 2.8 miles to a rocky, rutted area. After some loose shale, ruts and rock dropoffs, the trail meets with Bloody Nose Trail. Take it left, downhill. You'll cross a creek at 3.2 miles and head uphill. You'll reach an area with good views at 3.6 miles, elevation 350'. After some sandy switchbacks and challenging descents you'll come to a picnic table in a eucalyptus grove at 4.1 miles. Keep going straight on the double track as it parallels Camp Keep. Stay on the dirt road, bearing right downhill to Pecho Valley Road. Turn right on Pecho Valley Road at 4.6 miles and return to the trailhead at 6.2 miles.

Bloody Nose Trail

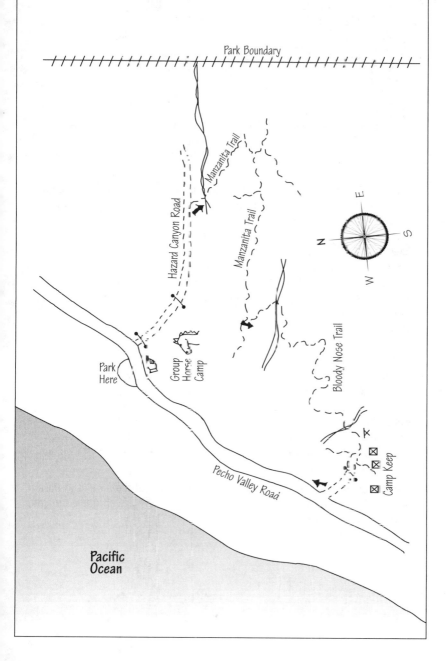

Upper Hazard Canyon

Difficulty: 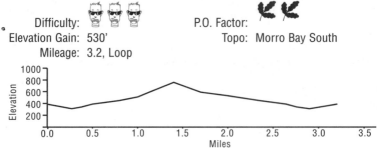   P.O. Factor:

Elevation Gain: 530'   Topo: Morro Bay South

Mileage: 3.2, Loop

This short but fun trail provides a good warm-up and good practice for new riders to develop skills for technical descents. If you don't have lots of time to ride or are doing multiple rides in Montana De Oro, this is a great addition.

Getting There

From San Luis Obispo or Highway 101, take Los Osos Valley Road through the town of Los Osos. Continuing on, the road becomes Pecho Valley Road. Pass the Montana De Oro entrance sign. Just over the crest of the hill, on the left, is a gate marked "Group Horse Camp." Park near the gate or in the dirt pullout just past it on the right.

The Ride

Bypass the steel gate and pedal down the road passing the horse camp on the right. Pass a second gate at 0.4 miles and go uphill. At 0.8 miles take Manzanita Trail to the right. Starting out as winding single track, the trail soon starts a long, steady climb uphill over a series of water bars. At 1.4 miles, turn left as the trail intersects with East Boundary. Soon you'll start a bumpy descent complete with ruts and lots of water bars. Running parallel to the park boundary fence, you'll cross a small creek at 1.7 miles.

The trail turns to double track around the 2-mile-point, at the far end of Hazard Canyon Road. You will pass Manzanita Trail at 2.4 miles. Keep going straight, returning to the trailhead, 3.2 miles.

Upper Hazard Canyon

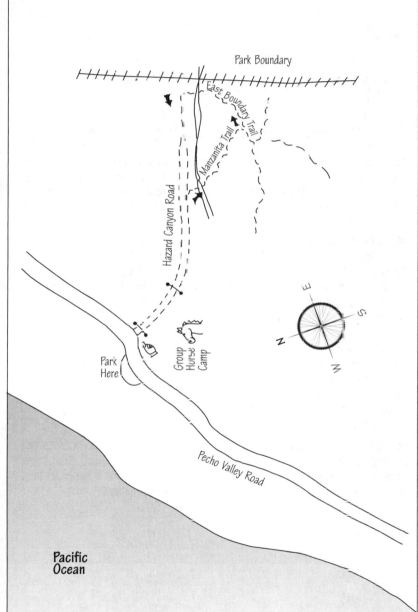

Bluff Trail

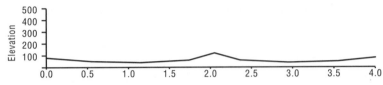

Difficulty:
Elevation Gain: 190'
Mileage: 4, Out-And-Back

P.O. Factor: Zilch
Topo: Morro Bay South

This wide and smooth trail is perfect for the greenhorn rider. Picturesque surroundings make for great picnics and resting spots. The flat terrain makes this
trail very popular with tourists out for leisurely strolls, so please be courteous.
This is the only trail open to bikes on the south side of the park. Let's not lose it!

Getting There

From San Luis Obispo or Highway 101, take Los Osos Valley Road through the
town of Los Osos. Continuing on, the road becomes Pecho Valley Road. Drive 2.7
miles past the Montana De Oro State Park entrance sign and park on the bluffs
overlooking Spooner's Cove. The trailhead, marked by a sign, is located at the
south end of the parking area.

The Ride

The trail starts out by dropping down from Pecho Valley Road and crossing a
wooden foot bridge. A trail splits off to the left toward Pecho Valley Road.
However, stay to the right as the trail heads westerly along the southern rim of
Spooner's Cove. Several smaller trails traverse across this trail. Just stay close to
the bluff as you head south.

At 1.6 miles follow the trail as it forks to the left. Just ahead the trails drops into
a small ravine. At about 2 miles the trail meets Pecho Valley Road. From here,
head back the way you came and return to the parking area at 4 miles. Or for a
shortcut, take Pecho Valley Road to reach the parking area at 3.2 miles.

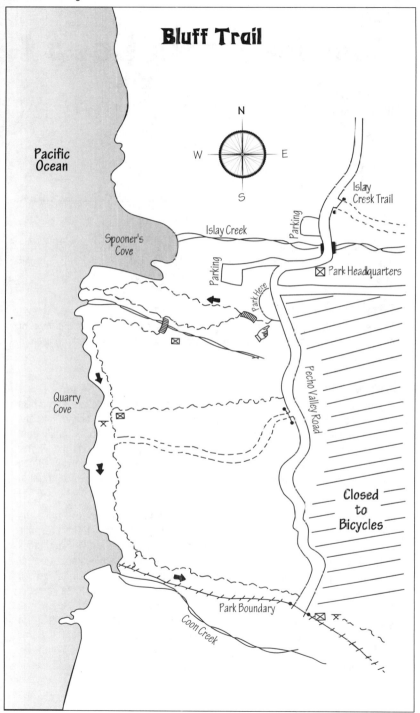

Cabrillo Peaks Loop 1

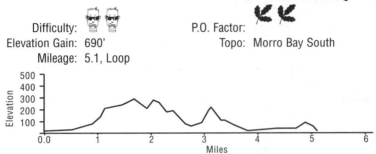

Difficulty: 😎 😎   P.O. Factor: ✔ ✔
Elevation Gain: 690'   Topo: Morro Bay South
Mileage: 5.1, Loop

Part of Morro Bay State Park, the Cabrillo Peaks area contains a large network of trails offering something for everyone. This is one suggested loop, but you can make up your own. The park is so small, it's nearly impossible to get lost.

Getting There

From San Luis Obispo or US 101, take Los Osos Valley Road toward the town of Los Osos. Turn right on South Bay Boulevard. Park in the large parking area at the second entrance to the park.

The Ride

Leaving the parking area, start pedaling north on South Bay Boulevard in the bike lane. At 0.5 miles turn right onto a road, bypassing a gate. Just ahead, take the single track heading uphill. At 0.9 miles, bear left at the "Y" heading uphill. Just over a mile into the ride another trail cuts left, but keep going straight on Quarry Trail. You will pass through a small gully and Live Oak Trail on the right. Keep going straight. After passing through another gully, take Park Ridge Trail right at 1.7 miles.

Upon reaching the saddle and four-way intersection at 2.0 miles turn right and then bear right. Just over a large rock slab take the single track right, downhill. Follow the trail right as it curves downhill. After dropping into a ravine and creek crossing, the trail joins Live Oak Trail. Take it left. After a series of water bars, bear left as the trail forks at 2.6 miles. Just ahead, take Park Ridge Trail left. At 3.0 miles, bear right onto Crespi Trail. Keep heading uphill until coming to an intersection with Chumash Trail. Turn right on Chumash and take it to Turri Road. Turn right on Turri Road and right again on South Bay Boulevard. At 4.7 miles turn right into the park's southern entrance. Take Live Oak Trail left, going uphill. Some small trails cut in from the right, but stay on Live Oak as it parallels South Bay Boulevard. Head toward some eucalyptus trees, dropping into the parking area at 5.1 miles.

Cabrillo Peaks Loop 1

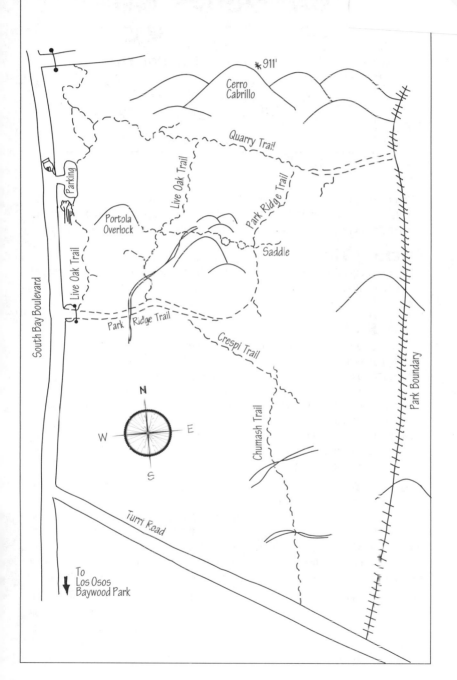

*911'

Cerro
Cabrillo

Quarry Trail

Live Oak Trail

Park Ridge Trail

Parking

Portola
Overlock

Saddle

Live Oak Trail

South Bay Boulevard

Park Ridge Trail

Crespi Trail

Chumash Trail

Park Boundary

N

W   E

S

Turri Road

To
Los Osos
Baywood Park

Cabrillo Peaks Loop 2

Difficulty: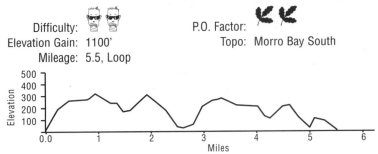
Elevation Gain: 1100'
Mileage: 5.5, Loop

P.O. Factor:
Topo: Morro Bay South

Part of Morro Bay State Park, the Cabrillo Peaks area contains a large network of trails offering something for everyone. This is one suggested loop, but you can make up your own. The park is so small, it's nearly impossible to get lost.

Getting There

From San Luis Obispo or US 101, take Los Osos Valley Road toward the town of Los Osos. Turn right on South Bay Boulevard. Park in the large parking area at the second entrance to the park.

The Ride

From the parking area, start up Quarry Trail. Various trails cut in from the left and right, but keep going straight on Quarry Trail. At 0.8 miles turn right onto a single track going uphill (a sign says To Park Ridge Trail). Just ahead, keep right as the trail splits. Soon you will come to an area called "the saddle." Continue straight ahead, crossing Park Ridge Trail. Just ahead, bear right as the trail splits. Just after crossing over a large rock slab, go right. Bear right again just ahead and descend through a gully. You will cross Live Oak Trail at 1.6 miles. Go straight as the trail climbs to Portola Overlook. An awesome view of the back bay and Morro Rock awaits at the top, elevation 329'.

Head back down the way you came joining Live Oak Trail at 2.3 miles. Turn right. After a descent over a series of water bars, bear left at the "Y" at 2.5 miles and again just ahead. Turn left onto Park Ridge Trail at 2.6 miles. Take Crespi Trail right at the fork just ahead. You will cross Chumash Trail at 3.0 miles as you continue straight on Crespi. At 3.2 miles bear right at the fork staying on Crespi. A small trail cuts in from the right, but stay on the main trail. You will cross a creek at 3.6 miles before starting to climb. There are great views at the top of a small hill at 4.1 miles.

Just past a gully, a small spur trail cuts right. But continue straight until you reach Chumash Trail at 4.5 miles. Turn right. Stay on Chumash until joining Park Ridge Trail. Turn left, going downhill. Stay on Park Ridge Trail until reaching Live Oak Trail. Take it right. Just ahead, veer left and continue going uphill. As you approach South Bay Boulevard, bear right and continue on to the parking area, 5.5 miles.

Cabrillo Peaks Loop 2

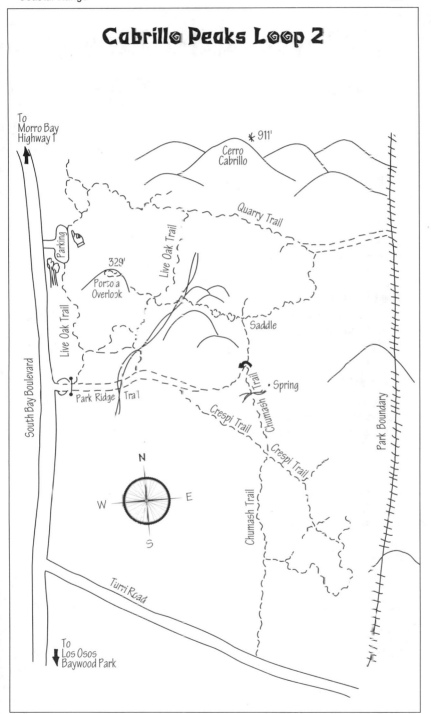

To
Morro Bay
Highway 1

* 911'
Cerro
Cabrillo

Quarry Trail

Parking

Live Oak Trail

329'
Portola
Overlook

Saddle

Live Oak Trail

Spring

Chumash Trail

South Bay Boulevard

Park Ridge Trail

Crespi Trail

Crespi Trail

Park Boundary

N
W   E
S

Chumash Trail

Turri Road

To
Los Osos
Baywood Park

Cerro Alto Loop

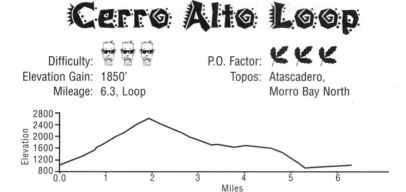

Difficulty: 👓👓👓   P.O. Factor: 🍂🍂🍂
Elevation Gain: 1850'   Topos: Atascadero,
Mileage: 6.3, Loop   Morro Bay North

While not real long on mileage, this trail offers the steepest climbing Cerro Alto has to offer. Most people will have to walk their bikes up several sections. Diehards can vie for king of the hill position. Get ready for cool descents.

Getting There

From San Luis Obispo take US 101 north and exit onto Highway 41. Take Highway 41 to Cerro Alto Campground, located about halfway between Morro Bay and Atascadero. Drive through the campground to the "Hikers & Bikers" parking area. The trailhead, marked by a small sign is located between campsites 16 and 17.

The Ride

Follow the single track as it drops down and crosses the east fork of Morro Creek on a wooden bridge. The climb gets very steep before coming to a "T" at the top of the steep section at 0.8 miles. Turn left 0.1 miles ahead. A sign says "Cerro Alto 1.2 miles." Turn right, uphill on the single track.

At 1.4 miles go left at the "Y." From here there are great views of Morro Rock and the Pacific Ocean. This section is a tough, steep climb. You will come to another intersection at 1.7 miles. Go left on the old jeep trail and continue climbing. You will reach the summit of Cerro Alto at 1.9 miles, elevation 2624'. Kick back for outstanding views in all directions.

Head back down the way you came. But when you reach the intersection at 2.2 miles, go straight this time. At 2.7 miles, go left at the fork continuing on the old jeep trail. Ride over a dirt mound and bypass a steel gate before dropping onto TV Tower Road at 2.8 miles. Turn right.

Continue straight as the AT&T Cable Route cuts right. Soon you will come to a eucalyptus grove. Keep going straight, staying to the left. Just ahead, go over a mound and enter a narrow alley of eucalyptus trees.

Bypass a pipe fence at 3.4 miles and keep going. Next comes a fun section of mounds. You will come to a four-way intersection at 3.8 miles. Go right, uphill on the switchback.

At 4.6 miles, take the single track downhill to the right. Get ready for a rocky, steep descent. After crossing a creek, the trail drops into poison oak heaven. You will come out at the road that runs through the campground at 5.5 miles. Turn right and return to your car, 6.3 miles.

Cerro Alto Loop

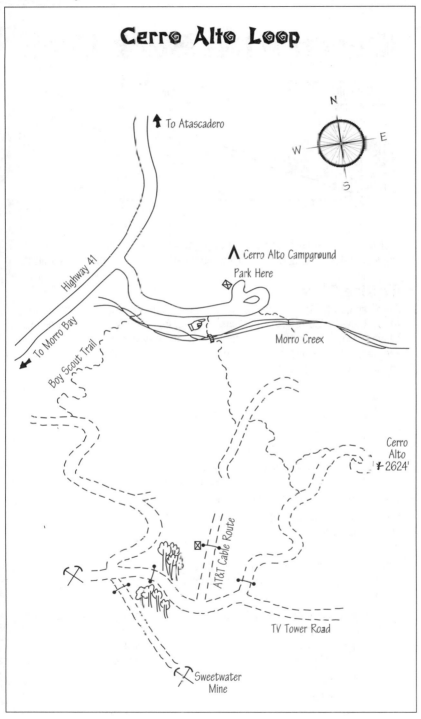

To Atascadero

N
W   E
S

Cerro Alto Campground
Park Here

Highway 41

To Morro Bay

Boy Scout Trail

Morro Creek

Cerro
Alto
2624'

AT&T Cable Route

TV Tower Road

Sweetwater
Mine

Cerro Alto Back Trail

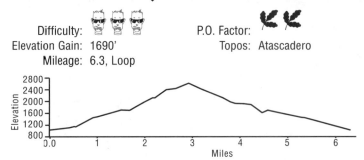

Difficulty: 😎😎😎   P.O. Factor: 🍂🍂

Elevation Gain: 1690'   Topos: Atascadero

Mileage: 6.3, Loop

Just remember, what goes up must come down. This ride has lots of climbing and lots of downhilling. Mostly on well groomed single track, this ride's a blast.

Getting There

From San Luis Obispo take US 101 north and exit onto Highway 41. Take Highway 41 west toward Morro Bay. Enter Cerro Alto Campground, located about halfway between Morro Bay and Atascadero. Drive all the way through the campground and park in the "Hikers & Bikers" parking area. The trailhead is at the southeast corner of the campground: Cerro Alto Trail #12E01.

The Ride

Start climbing immediately on nice, smooth single track. Within a half mile, you'll make a couple of creek crossings. Just under a mile, you will come out at a double track. Take it right uphill.

Just ahead at the next junction, bear left on the single track which climbs the hill more gradually. At 1.7 miles follow the trail sign uphill toward Cerro Alto. At 2.2 miles go straight at the junction. Just ahead at the next fork, turn left uphill.

Keep climbing, going straight at the junction at 2.7 miles (a trail descends left.) The trail now gets loose and rocky. You'll reach the top of Cerro Alto just under 3 miles, elevation 2624'.

When you're ready to head back down, go straight at the junction (the same way you came up). At 3.7 miles, go left at the junction. Bypass a steel gate just before joining TV Tower Road. Turn right.

At 3.9 miles turn right onto the AT&T cable route. Just ahead, go straight at the fork bypassing a steel gate. (A small building sits left.) You'll start a big descent at 4.2 miles. At 4.5 miles, keep going straight at the fork. You'll arrive back at the trail sign marked "Cerro Alto 1.2 miles" at 4.6 miles. Keep going straight for a fast descent.

At 5.3 miles, bear right at the "Y" then bear left on the single track just ahead, going downhill. Return to the trailhead, 6.3 miles.

Cerro Alto Back Trail

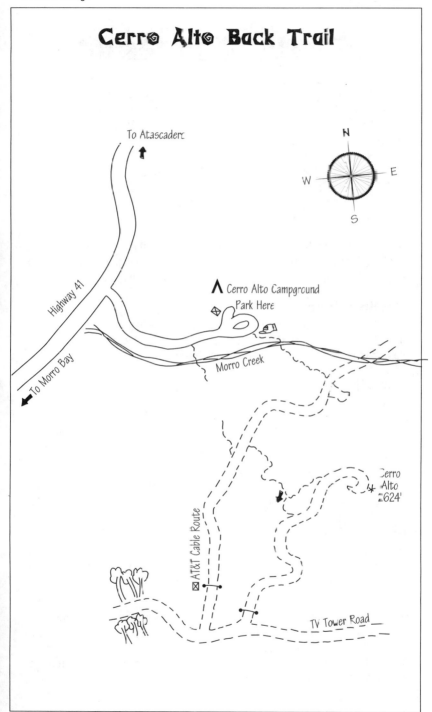

To Atascadero

Highway 41

To Morro Bay

Cerro Alto Campground
Park Here

Morro Creek

AT&T Cable Route

Cerro
Alto
2624'

TV Tower Road

Santa Rita Road

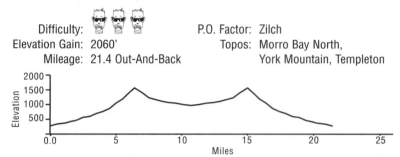

Difficulty: 👤👤👤   P.O. Factor: Zilch
Elevation Gain: 2060'   Topos: Morro Bay North,
Mileage: 21.4 Out-And-Back   York Mountain, Templeton

Starting at the north end of Whale Rock Reservoir, this country road (a.k.a. Cayucos Templeton Road) snakes through narrow canyons and climbs over Oak Ridge. Entirely on dirt and paved road, this is a great training ride.

Getting There

From San Luis Obispo, take Highway 1 north for 17.5 miles. Just before the town of Cayucos, turn right on Old Creek Road. Take it 3.8 miles to Santa Rita Road, the first road on the right past Whale Rock Reservoir. Park in the dirt pullout.

The Ride

Pedal up Santa Rita Road. It turns to dirt just 1.2 miles ahead. When the road splits at 2.8 miles, bear left continuing on Santa Rita Road. The road starts to steepen at 4 miles, winding its way up the canyon. At 5.1 miles you will break through the trees as you climb across Oak Ridge.

The high point, elevation 1530' is reached at 6.4 miles. From this mountain vista, you can see the northern Santa Lucia Mountains, the Pacific Ocean and regions inland. Continuing toward Templeton, a long winding descent brings you alongside Santa Rita Creek at 7.5 miles. The road heads downhill gradually for the next several miles as it snakes through a narrow canyon following the creek.

At 10.1 miles, the road is paved for a short while before becoming dirt again. At 10.7 miles the road returns to pavement. A stone wall and dirt pullout is on the left. Turn around here and head back the way you came, returning to your car at 21.4 miles.

For a longer ride, keep going toward Templeton. You will start a short climb upon passing the entrance to "Rancho Oak View" at 12.5 miles. Just ahead Raymond Avenue cuts right, but keep going straight. You will cross a bridge at 14.1 miles. Santa Rita Road curves to the left before reaching Vineyard Drive at 14.9 miles. Turn right and head into Templeton. You'll reach US 101 at 15.3 miles.

Santa Rita Road

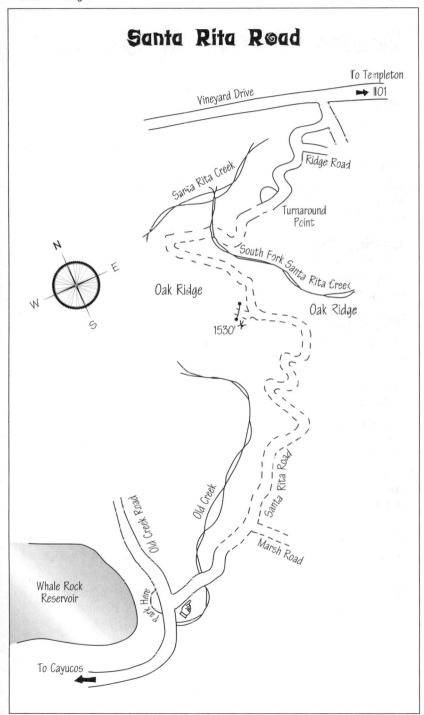

Pismo Beach & Oceano

Difficulty: 😎 😎   P.O. Factor: Zilch
Elevation Gain: Negligible   Topo: Oceano
Mileage: 20, Out-And-Back

This is a ride for beach lovers! Put on your shades and sunscreen and do it! Much of this ride is open to motor vehicles so pay attention.

Helpful Tips: Deflate your tires to about 30 psi for a wider "footprint" and rinse off your bike and relube the drive train when you get home. And one more thing—don't go in the water on your bike.

Getting There

From San Luis Obispo take US 101 south for 11 miles and exit on Highway 1. Follow Highway 1 as it continues south. Turn right on Grand Avenue, following the sign that says "Beach Ramp." Park in the lot.

The Ride

From the parking lot, pass the toll booth and head down the ramp to the beach. Pedal to the south along the water's edge, where the sand is the firmest. Since there are only two ramps to service the entire area, they get a lot of use, so be careful of vehicles. The Oceano Ramp drops onto the beach at 1.2 miles and can be used as an alternative trailhead.

The designated camping area begins at 2.1 miles and continues for several miles. The vehicle boundary fence at 5.6 miles marks the end of the off-road vehicle area. Hop over the fence and continue as the sand becomes a bit softer.

At 6.5 miles Oso Flaco Creek flows into the ocean. Leave your bike on the beach and explore the estuary. You will be rewarded with a glimpse at a very fragile and rare ecosystem. If you go back far enough you will join the Nipomo Dunes Trail that leads to Oso Flaco Lake.

Once back on your bike, cross the small creek and continue south. You will reach the UNOCAL Guadalupe Oil Field at 9.8 miles. Pedal on another 0.2 miles before turning around to make the ride an even 20 miles.

On the return trip you will hop the fence at 14.4 miles. Pass the Oceano Ramp at 18.7 miles and reach the top of the Grand Avenue Ramp at 20 miles.

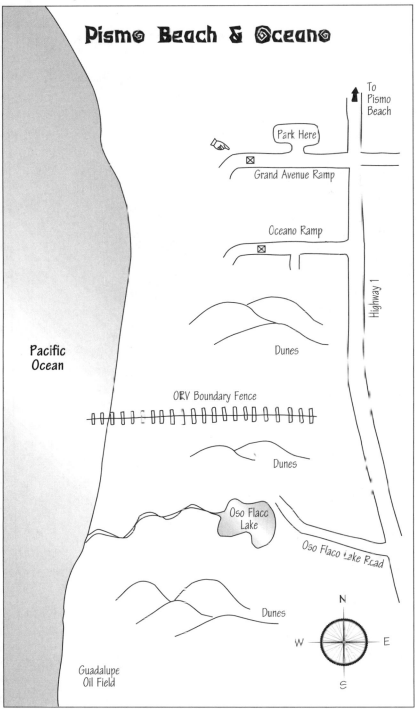

Pismo Beach & Oceano

To Pismo Beach

Park Here

Grand Avenue Ramp

Oceano Ramp

Highway 1

Pacific Ocean

Dunes

ORV Boundary Fence

Dunes

Oso Flaco Lake

Oso Flaco Lake Road

Dunes

Guadalupe Oil Field

N
W   E
S

North County

North County Overview

Within the county, San Luis Obispo usually gets most of the glory. But when it comes to mountain biking, the north county offers the most in pure, unadulterated adventure! It is here that the most advanced trails are found.

If you're gonzo, get to Pozo. Not much has changed around this tiny townsite in the past 100 years. That's great for mountain bikers as you truly can get away from it all. In general, the trails in this area are best suited for intermediate, advanced and crazy riders. Plan on spending several hours to complete most rides. Tip: If you're in Pozo Thursday through Sunday, make a stop at the Pozo Saloon for great grub (call ahead to confirm hours). The Saloon also has live music on most Sundays. We love this place!

Closer in is Santa Margarita Lake. The trails here are shorter in length, but lots of fun and very picturesque.

We also include a few trails in Paso Robles and Atascadero. Off the beaten path, these outstanding trails pass through ranching areas on the outskirts of town.

Weather in the northern part of the county tends to be more extreme: either hot and dry or cold and wet. You must take lots of extra water in the hot months and remember to bring protective clothing in the wet months. Pozo in particular is sparse on services, so travel self-contained.

North County Overview

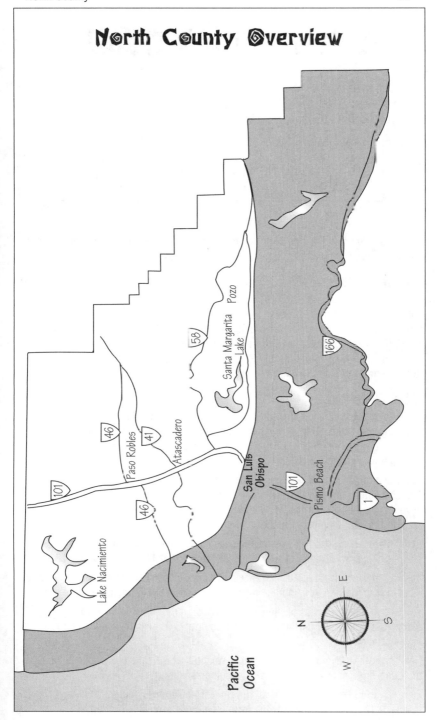

Blinn Ranch Trail

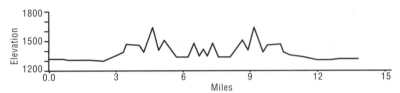

Difficulty: P.O. Factor: Zilch
Elevation Gain: 1820'   Topo: Santa Margarita Lake
Mileage: 13.8, Out-And-Back

This is a great training ride with some challenging climbs and many vistas of Santa Margarita Lake and its surrounding rock formations.

Getting There

From San Luis Obispo take US 101 north and exit at Highway 58/Santa Margarita. Follow Highway 58 through town, crossing the railroad tracks. When Highway 58 forks to the left, continue straight on Pozo Road. Pass the signs to Santa Margarita Lake, continuing on Pozo Road. Just after crossing a bridge, take River Road left, following the signs to "River Road Access." Park in the River Road Access Parking Area. There is a fee to park here.

The Ride

Go through the gate and follow the trail about a half mile until reaching a fork. Go right on Blinn Ranch Trail (Sandstone Trail goes left). You will pass an old building on the right before a creek crossing. Bear left at the "Y" and follow the trail sign, passing through a gate.

You will come alongside a finger of the lake at about 1.2 miles. Pass an old pen near the water's edge and begin a short climb. You will make a very wide crossing of Alamo Creek at 1.8 miles. At 3.3 miles, you will pass a sign for Cold Canyon Trail on the left. Keep going straight on the road.

At 4.2 miles you have to hike around a washed out section of road. Back on your bike, start a climb, passing a gate at the high point of the ride at 4.6 miles, elevation 1640'.

Pass another washout at about 5 miles. The road descends before coming to a quiet inlet of the lake. At about 6.1 miles you will see a boat ramp across the lake.

You will complete a series of climbs and descents, again drawing near to the lake. Climb to a gate which is the turnaround point at 6.9 miles. Private property is beyond the gate.

Head back the way you came, passing a washout at 8.8 miles. You'll be back at the ride's high point at 9.1 miles and the other washout at 9.6 miles.

Pass the Cold Canyon trailhead at 10.5 miles. You'll cross Alamo Creek at 11.8 miles. At 13 miles turn right at the fork, then cross a creek. Turn left at the "Y" continuing on Blinn Ranch Trail. Arrive back at the car at 13.8 miles.

Blinn Ranch Trail

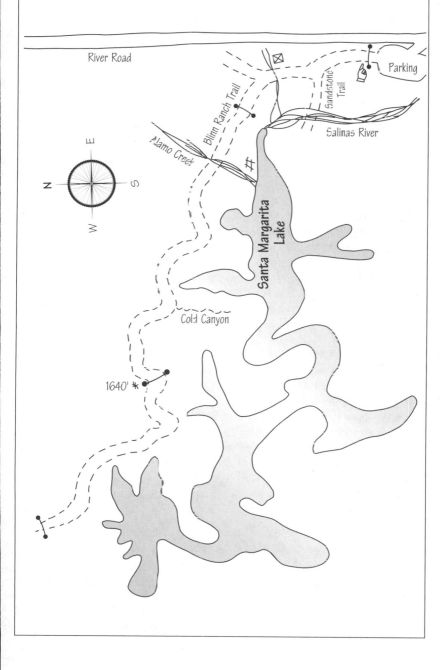

River Road

Blinn Ranch Trail

Sandstone Trail

Parking

Salinas River

Alamo Creek

Santa Margarita Lake

Cold Canyon

1640'

Cold Canyon

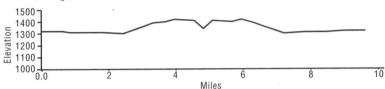

Difficulty: 👹 👹 👹   P.O. Factor: Zilch
Elevation Gain: 610'   Topo: Santa Margarita Lake
Mileage: 9.6, Out-And-Back

This is a scenic ride with lots of variety. The fun single track is a training ground for perfecting your technical performance.

Getting There

From San Luis Obispo take US 101 north and exit at Highway 58/Santa Margarita. Follow Highway 58 through town, crossing the railroad tracks. When Highway 58 forks to the left, continue straight on Pozo Road. Keep going on Pozo Road for about 16 miles. Along the way, you will pass signs to Santa Margarita Lake. Just after crossing a bridge, take River Road left, following the sign to "River Road Access." Park in the River Road Access Parking Area. There is a fee to park here.

The Ride

Go through and follow the trail about a half mile until reaching a fork. Go right on Blinn Ranch Trail (Sandstone Trail goes left). You will pass an old building on the right before crossing a stream. A road splits right, but keep going straight. Follow the trail sign, passing through a gate.

You will come alongside a finger of the lake at 1.2 miles. Pass an old pen near the water's edge and begin a short climb. You will make a wide crossing of Alamo Creek at 1.8 miles. Follow the trail until you come to a sign for Cold Canyon Trail at 3.3 miles. Take the single track to the left. This is a fun middle chain ring cruiser.

At 3.7 miles you will come to a fork. Turn right, following the sign toward Sapwi Camp. (Going straight 0.10 miles heads to the Horse Camp where there is a picnic table and pit toilet.)

You will encounter lots of fun switchbacks before arriving at Sapwi Camp at 4.8 miles. This is the turnaround point and a great place to rest or picnic.

Head back the way you came, arriving at the fork to Horse Camp at just under 6 miles. Turn left, coming out of Cold Canyon at 6.3 miles. Turn right on Blinn Ranch Trail. You will cross Alamo Creek at 6.4 miles. At 9 miles turn right at the fork, cross the creek and pass an old building. At 9.1 miles turn left at the fork (Sandstone Trail goes right) and return to your car 9.6 miles.

Cold Canyon

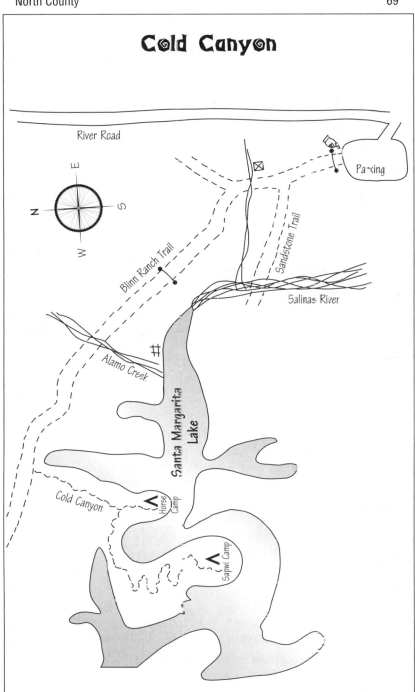

Sandstone Trail

Difficulty: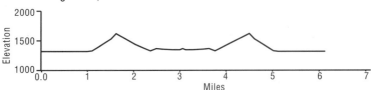

Difficulty:	P.O. Factor: Zilch
Elevation Gain: 710'	Topo: Santa Margarita Lake
Mileage: 6.1, Out-And-Back	

If you don't mind getting your feet wet, you'll enjoy this picturesque ride through the back reaches of Santa Margarita Lake.

Getting There

From San Luis Obispo take US 101 north and exit at Highway 58/Santa Margarita. Follow Highway 58 through town, crossing the railroad tracks. When Highway 58 forks to the left, continue straight on Pozo Road. Keep going on Pozo Road for about 16 miles. Along the way, you will pass signs to Santa Margarita Lake. Just after crossing a bridge, take River Road left, following the sign to "River Road Access." Park in the River Road Access Parking Area. There is a fee to park here.

The Ride

Go through the gate and follow the trail about a half mile until reaching a fork. Go left on Sandstone Trail (Blinn Ranch Trail goes right). Just ahead cross the Salinas River. This is a very deep river crossing (sometimes as deep as 4 feet). Carry your bike across. Continue on the trail which is now a faint double track.

At about 1.1 miles, the trail bends left and starts to climb up a canyon. You'll reach the top of the climb at 1.6 miles, elevation 1620'. Now start your long descent. You'll pass a large rock formation on the left (and waterfall during the wet season) at 2.4 miles. The lake is on the right.

Carry your bike over a broken cement bridge at 2.6 miles. Back on your bike, continue straight, uphill.

You will cross a small creek at 2.8 miles followed shortly by two others. At 3 miles you make your fourth creek crossing. Just ahead, you will come to a locked gate marking the end of the San Luis Obispo County Recreation Area. Turn around here.

Cross the broken cement bridge at 3.5 miles and the ride's high point at 4.5 miles, elevation 1620'. Cross the Salinas River at 5.6 miles. Just ahead bear right at the "Y" and return to the trailhead at 6.1 miles.

Sandstone Trail

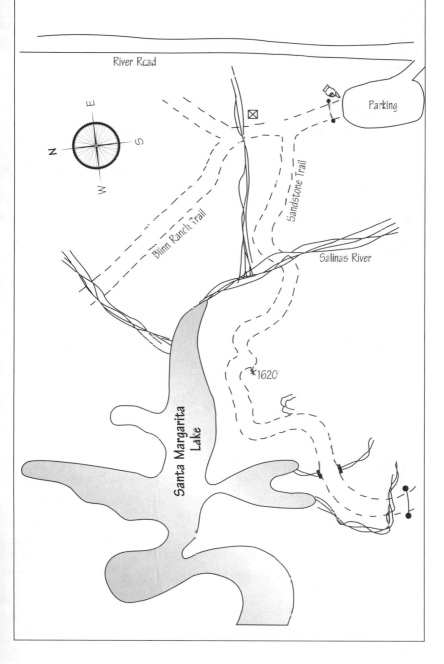

River Road

E
N · S
W

Parking

Sandstone Trail

Blinn Ranch Trail

Salinas River

*1620'

Santa Margarita Lake

Rinconada Trail

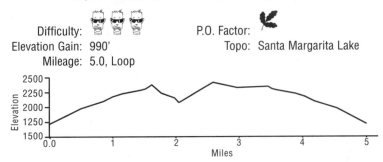

Difficulty:

Elevation Gain: 990'

Mileage: 5.0, Loop

P.O. Factor:

Topo: Santa Margarita Lake

This is a fun trail running through past and present mining areas. The single track twists through loose, rocky climbs and descents.

Getting There

From San Luis Obispo take US 101 north and exit at Highway 58/Santa Margarita. Follow Highway 58 through town, crossing the railroad tracks. When Highway 58 forks to the left, continue straight on Pozo Road. Drive another 9.8 miles until you see a sign marking the trail. Pull up the driveway and park.

The Ride

Follow the trail as it gently climbs the grassy hills. The single track winds around, then climbs steeply to a vista point where you can catch a glimpse of the Rinconada Mine to the northwest. At 1 mile, go right at the "T" then left following the trail sign.

Now on double track, take the single track that cuts left just before a gate at 1.4 miles. When you come off the single track, take the dirt road right. You will arrive at the "saddle" area at about 1.6 miles. Go left, downhill following the "Trail" sign.

After a loose, rocky descent, continue straight, following the sign. (A single track heads to a trough on the left and a double track goes right.) After a steep and bumpy descent you will drop onto Hi Mountain Lookout Road at 2 miles. Go left.

The road forks at 3 miles. Take the jeep road to the left. At 3.4 miles, take the single track cutting right (this is the trail you were on earlier).

Once back on double track, head right, downhill. At 4 miles, turn left at the fork onto single track. You'll be back at the trailhead at 5 miles.

(For a longer version of this ride, turn the page.)

Rinconada Trail

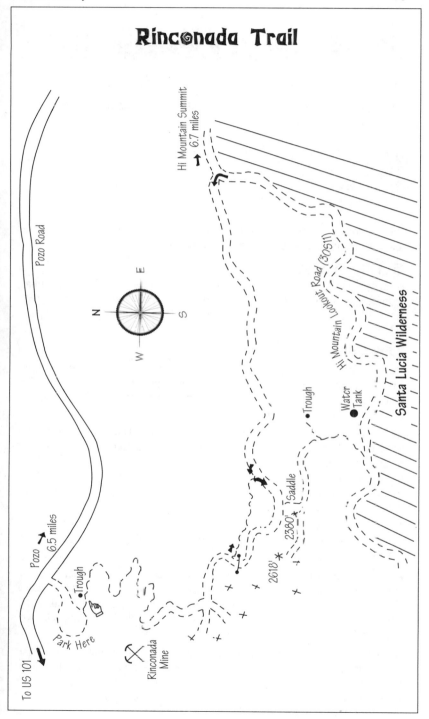

To US 101

Pozo
6.5 miles

Pozo Road

Park Here

•Trough

Rinconada
Mine

N
E
W
S

Hi Mountain Summit
6.7 miles

Santa Lucia Wilderness

Hi Mountain Lookout Road (30S11)

•Trough

Water
Tank

Saddle

2380'

2618'

Hi Mountain Lookout RD.

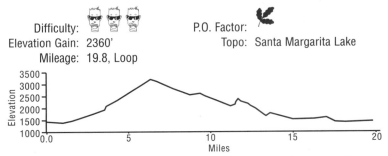

Difficulty: P.O. Factor:

Elevation Gain: 2360'   Topo: Santa Margarita Lake

Mileage: 19.8, Loop

This trail requires intermediate-level riding skills and stamina. Long climbs are rewarded by great views and some fun, twisty single track.

Getting There

From San Luis Obispo take US 101 north and exit at Highway 58/Santa Margarita. Follow Highway 58 through town, crossing the railroad tracks. When Highway 58 forks to the left, continue straight on Pozo Road. Drive another 17 miles and park near the ranger station.

The Ride

From the ranger station, pedal up Hi Mountain Road, which immediate turns to dirt. You will cross the Salinas River at the 1-mile-mark and then a small creek. The road begins climbing shortly after entering the Los Padres National Forest. It's mostly uphill for the next couple of miles.

At 3.6 miles you will reach Hi Mountain Summit, 2080'. Follow the sign toward Hi Mountain Lookout. You will pass the Hi Mountain Campground at 4.3 miles. Keep climbing until reaching the top of the ridge at 5.9 miles. Turn left, going through a gate to reach Hi Mountain Lookout (if you want to skip this brief side trip, turn right). After taking in the great views from the lookout, continue on as the road descends.

At 7.7 miles follow a big sweeping switchback to the right. Soon you will pass the Mercury Belle trailhead. Keep going. The road soon begins steadily climbing. At 9.3 miles a road cuts left, but stay on the main road. Continue on, going downhill.

At 10.3 miles, you'll come to a "Y." Going right is a shortcut, but veer left if you're still going strong. Around the bend, take the single track uphill marked "Rinconada Trailhead 2 mi." At the top of the climb, bear right on the steep, loose single track. You'll come to a "Y" at 11.5 miles. Bear left, uphill following a brown trail sign (a water trough is on the right).

At the top of the climb you will come to a saddle. Turn right onto a jeep trail. Just ahead, turn left onto a single track. You'll drop onto a jeep trail at 11.8 miles. Turn right. Soon you will take a single track downhill at the fork. Follow the single track as it switchbacks down the parking area for Rinconada Trail. At 13.3 miles turn right onto Pozo Road. The ride back to the car is all on paved road, 19.8 miles.

Hi Mountain Lookout Road

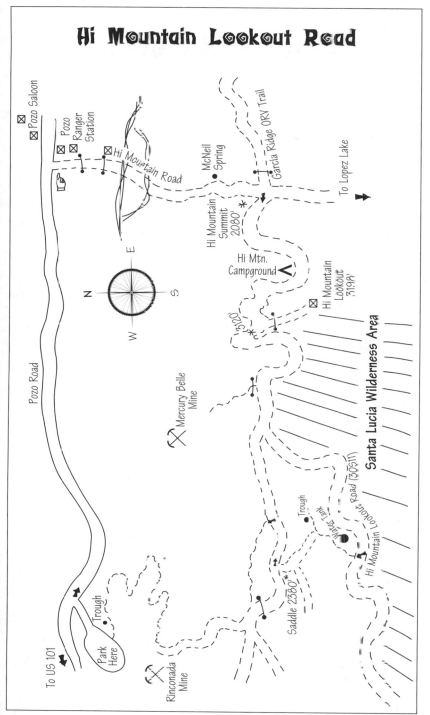

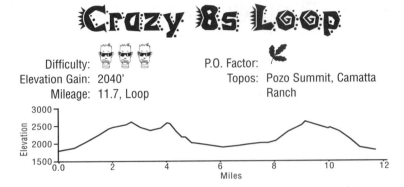

Crazy 8s Loop

Difficulty: 😎 😎 😎

P.O. Factor: 🐾

Elevation Gain: 2040'
Mileage: 11.7, Loop

Topos: Pozo Summit, Camatta Ranch

This trail has a little bit of everything—both gradual and steep climbs, flats and some rock'n' descents on ORV trails.

Getting There

From San Luis Obispo take US 101 north and exit at Highway 58/Santa Margarita. Follow Highway 58 through town, crossing the railroad tracks. When Highway 58 forks to the left, continue straight on Pozo Road. You will reach Pozo in about 17 miles. Go through town and take Parkhill Road when it intersects with Pozo Road. (Pozo Road cuts right.) In about 3 miles, turn right on Navajo Grade Road. Just ahead is the Turkey Flat ORV staging area. Park there.

The Ride

From Turkey Flat, pedal east up Navajo Grade Road (29S02). Take it 2.7 miles to "5 Points" intersection. Take the center road downhill toward Friis Camp. Continue on the road as it curves left at 3 miles (ignore the road cutting right). At 3.4 miles, Navajo Bypass Trail #15 splits to the right. Take it, crossing a creek. The trail winds through a meadow before climbing.

At 4.1 miles make a steep downhill, turning left of the transmission tower. Just ahead are some very steep sections topped with concrete blocks (for much needed traction). Continue as the trail becomes a wide, sandy double track. At 4.7 miles, turn right, heading downhill. (A green gate is uphill to the left.)

You will come out at McGinnis Creek Road turn left. Just ahead, take McGinnis Creek Trail #17(16E14) which is marked by a sign at about 5 miles. This single track provides lots of fun little ups and downs as it follows alongside the creek. Soon you will see McGinnis Creek Road to the right. But stay on the single track as it crosses the stream. After going through a gate, the single track ends at a dirt road at 6.2 miles. Turn right, cross McGinnis Creek and following what is now McGinnis Creek Road.

Stay on McGinnis Creek Road, passing the sign for McGinnis Creek Trail #17 at 7.5 miles. Pass Navajo Campground at 8 miles and arrive back at 5 Points at 9.1 miles.

Go downhill on pavement. At just under 10 miles, take the well-worn single track climbing to the left. At the top, go straight heading downhill. Stay on this main trail, following the "route" or "trail" signs. This section rocks! There's plenty of opportunity for air!

The trail ends at pavement. Turn left, returning to Turkey Flat at 11.7 miles.

Crazy 8s Loop

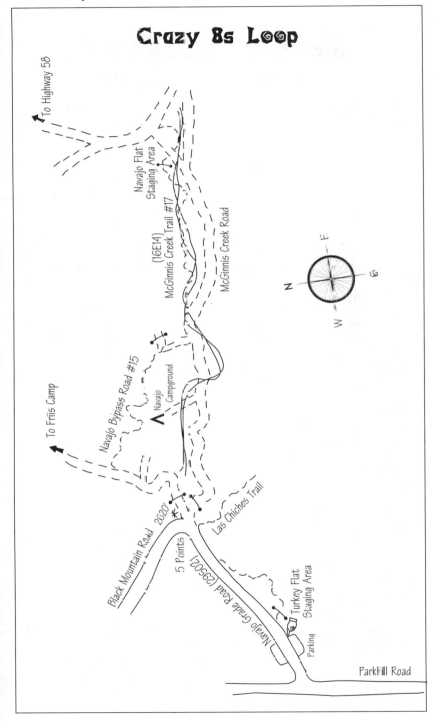

To Highway 58

Navajo Flat Staging Area

(10E14) McGinnis Creek Trail #17

McGinnis Creek Road

Navajo Bypass Road #15

Navajo Campground

To Friis Camp

Black Mountain Road 2620'

5 Points

Las Chiches Trail

Navajo Grade Road (2950.2)

Turkey Flat Staging Area

Parking

Parkhill Road

Fernandez Trail

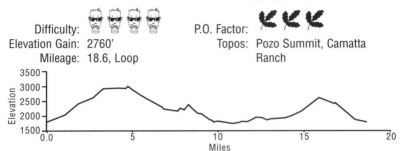

Difficulty: 🕶️🕶️🕶️🕶️   P.O. Factor: 🐦🐦🐦
Elevation Gain: 2760'   Topos: Pozo Summit, Camatta
Mileage: 18.6, Loop   Ranch

When this trail is not overgrown with poison oak and brush, it's one of the best single tracks the county has to offer. When it gets unruly, it's a drag. Check trail conditions through the Pozo Ranger station or take a chance—it's usually well worth the risk.

Getting There

From San Luis Obispo take US 101 north and exit at Highway 58/Santa Margarita. Follow Highway 58 through town, crossing the railroad tracks. When Highway 58 forks to the left, continue straight on Pozo Road. You will reach Pozo in about 17 miles. Go through town and take Parkhill Road when it intersects with Pozo Road. (Pozo Road cuts right.) In about 3 miles, turn right on Navajo Grade Road (29S02). Just ahead is the Turkey Flat ORV staging area. Park there.

The Ride

From Turkey Flat, follow the paved road. Take it 2.7 miles to the "5 Points" intersection. Go left, uphill on Black Mountain Road. The road climbs steeply then follows the ridge line. At 5 miles take the trail marked "Friis Camp 2 mi."

Follow this fun single track as it heads mostly downhill until reaching a motor vehicle stop and Friis Camp at 6.8 miles. A steel tank is just ahead on the left. Continue along the creek bottom crossing a jeep road. Pick up the single track again next to a second motor vehicle stop near the creek.

The single track now makes several creek crossings. The trail starts climbing to the right, away from the creek at 7.6 miles. You'll reach the top of this climb at 7.8 miles. Now descend on a series of switchbacks.

Start another climb, reaching the top at 8.3 miles, elevation 2380'. Continue straight downhill on the single track. (Fire breaks climb to the left and right.)

At 9.1 miles, bear right at the fork going downhill. Follow along the creek. At 9.2 miles you will come to motor vehicle stop. You'll see a road on the left. But continue on the single track as it continues along the creek and joins Fernandez Road just ahead. Turn right.

At 10.8 miles, the road from Bethel Ranch joins from the left. Continue straight. Pass a cattle guard and a block house at 11.4 miles. You will reach an intersection at 12.2 miles. Continue straight, downhill, merging onto McGinnis Creek Road.

At 12.9 miles you will reach the Navajo Flat staging area. Turn right and pedal through it,

Fernandez Trail

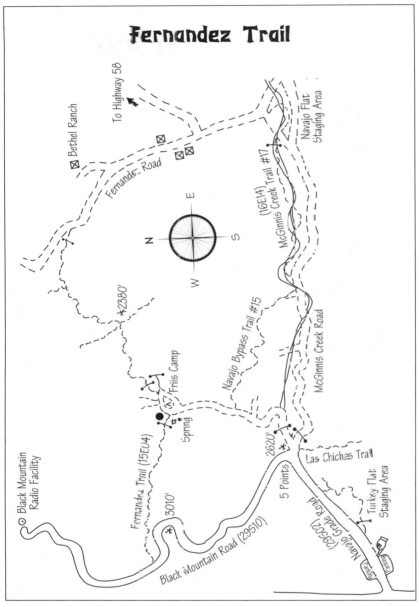

paralleling a steel pipe fence. At the "Y" just ahead, bear right onto McGinnis Creek Trail #17(16E14). (If you're tired, take the easy way on the road to the left.) Just ahead, go through a gate. Turn right as you rejoin McGinnis Creek Road at 14.3 miles.

Pass Navajo Campground on the right at 14.8 miles. Climb up to "5 Points" at 15.9 miles. Now head downhill on the paved road. At 16.8 miles, take the well worn single track uphill. At the top, bear right at the fork. Follow the "Route" and "Trail" signs.

You will reach pavement at 17.8 miles. Turn left, returning to Turkey Flat staging area, 18.6 miles.

Garcia Ridge

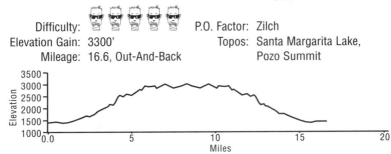

Difficulty: 👓 👓 👓 👓 👓   P.O. Factor: Zilch
Elevation Gain: 3300'   Topos: Santa Margarita Lake,
     Mileage: 16.6, Out-And-Back   Pozo Summit

This ride is for the climbers! Even if you consider yourself a mountain biking god, this trail will humble you. But don't take our word for it; check it out!

Getting There

From San Luis Obispo take US 101 north and exit at Highway 58/Santa Margarita. Follow Highway 58 through town, crossing the railroad tracks. When Highway 58 forks to the left, continue straight on Pozo Road. Drive another 17 miles to Pozo and park at the ranger station.

The Ride

Starting from the Pozo Ranger Station, head south on Hi Mountain Road, which immediately turns to dirt. You will cross the Salinas River at the one-mile-mark and then another creek crossing. The road begins climbing shortly after entering the Los Padres National Forest. It's mostly uphill for the next couple miles.

At 3.6 miles, you will reach Hi Mountain Summit. Garcia Ridge ORV Trail is on the left marked by a small metal sign. Take it. The next 0.5 miles include some of the hardest climbs this ride has to offer! You will be doing some walking in this first section.

After a brief plateau, start climbing again, finishing this monster climb at 4.2 miles. Descend, going right at the fork just ahead. After another short climb, you will descend with some great views in all directions. At 5 miles you will be at the base of another gnarly hill. Climb it then get ready for another long, tough climb.

Begin a steep, nasty downhill at 6.4 miles. You'll pass some cool rock formations at 6.6. Just ahead, go right at the fork (a vista point is to the left). Tackle a couple more steep climbs before arriving at the turnaround point at 8.3 miles, elevation 3030'. The trail ends at a turnaround and a steel pipe fence. Wilderness Area starts just beyond. If you need a rest, there's a picnic table under some trees.

Head back the way you came, reaching Hi Mountain Summit at 13.1 miles. Turn right, heading downhill arriving at the Pozo Ranger Station at 16.6 miles. Now stop crying and go home to mama.

Garcia Ridge

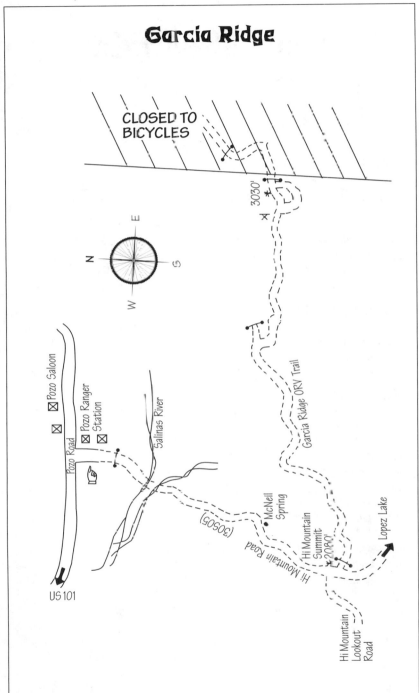

CLOSED TO
BICYCLES

3030'

Garcia Ridge ORV Trail

Pozo Saloon

Pozo Ranger
Station

Pozo Road

Salinas River

McNeil
Spring

Hi Mountain
Summit
2980'

Lopez Lake

Hi Mountain Road

(3050')

Hi Mountain
Lookout
Road

US 101

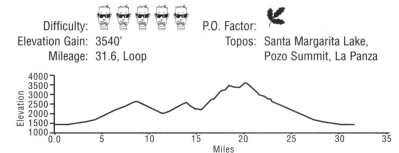

Pine Mountain

Difficulty: 👹 👹 👹 👹 👹   P.O. Factor: 🌿

Elevation Gain: 3540'   Topos: Santa Margarita Lake,
Mileage: 31.6, Loop   Pozo Summit, La Panza

This long ride challenges even the strongest riders. Its steep and loose uphills on Pine Ridge and two technical downhill sections known as "The Stair Steps" are the highlights of this ride. It offers 360° views which include Castle Crags and a bird's-eye view of California condors reintroduced to the area.

Getting There

From San Luis Obispo take US 101 north and exit at Highway 58/Santa Margarita. Follow Highway 58 through town, crossing the railroad tracks. When Highway 58 forks to the left, continue straight on Pozo Road. You will reach Pozo in about 17 miles. Park near the Pozo Saloon.

The Ride

From the Pozo Saloon head east on Pozo Road. When you come to the junction with Parkhill Road at 1.4 miles, turn right continuing on Pozo Road. Turn left at the junction with San Jose Avenales Ranch Road at 3.3 miles. Follow Pozo Road over a cement bridge (there's a dirt parking area here if you want a shorter ride). The road soon turns to dirt and climbs. You will reach Pozo Summit at 8.7 miles. Continue following Pozo Road on a long descent.

You will come to another junction at 11.6 miles. Turn right toward La Panza Campground and Highway 58. At 13.6 miles you will reach La Panza Summit, 2496'. Bear right at the "Y" toward Queen Bee Campground. Cross the cattle guard and descend through the campground.

At 15.9 miles, turn right at the fork, climbing Pine Mountain Road #8 (30S14). There's at least a half-mile of steep climbing. At 17.6 miles, the trail makes a sharp switchback to the right. Just after a motor vehicle stop on the left you'll come to a great spot to watch the condors.

At 18.5 miles you finally reach the top of the ridge. The road now follows the spine of Pine Mountain with many steep and challenging climbs and descents. At 20.6 miles you'll come to a junction. Go right, downhill. This is Pine Mountain Trail #7 (16E01) which takes you through the Stair Steps—the best part of the ride! At 21.4 miles, start the Stair Steps.

You will return to Pozo Summit at 22.9 miles. Now descend to Pozo. You will reach pavement at 27.4 miles. Continue on, meeting Parkhill Road at 30.2 miles. Follow Pozo Road, retracing your route and arriving back at the Saloon at 31.6 miles.

Pine Mountain

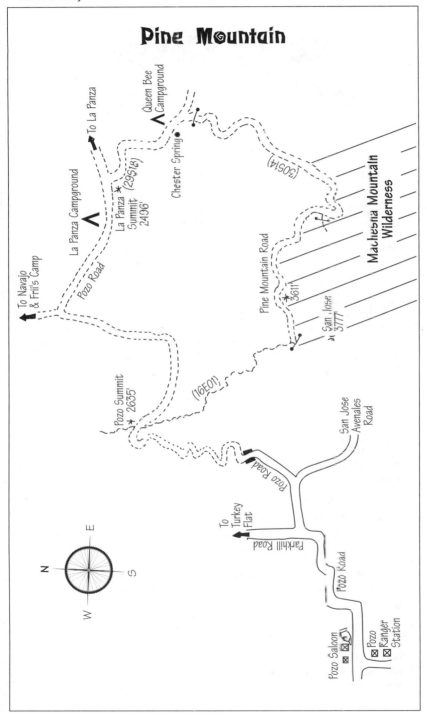

Rocky Canyon

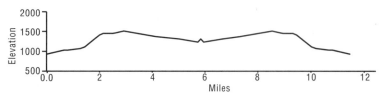

Difficulty: P.O. Factor: Zilch
Elevation Gain: 980'   Topo: Santa Margarita
Mileage: 11.5, Out-And-Back

Erosion and washouts turned this road into an area that is now off limits to cars. It's a great place for bikers, hikers and equestrians to enjoy a leisurely day in the country—and it's just on the outskirts of town.

Getting There

From San Luis Obispo take US 101 north and exit at San Diego Road in Atascadero. Follow it right off the freeway, then turn right on El Camino Real. Pass the entrance to the Atascadero State Mental Hospital and turn left on Viejo Camino. Turn left on Halcon Road which soon turns to dirt and crosses the Salinas River. Just ahead, you will come to a wide intersection with Rocky Canyon Road. Park here and start your ride just beyond a steel gate. (Rocky Canyon Road is closed to motor vehicles.)

The Ride

Pedal up the dirt road. You will enter an active Quarry at about 0.8 miles. Green and white "Rocky Canyon Trail" signs guide your way through the quarry.

Turn right at the fork at 1.3 miles and cross a creek. (Left is private property.) Crossing another creek bottom the trail turns to single track and climbs.

You will reach the top of the climb at 2.1 miles, 1450'. Now, parallel the fence. Just ahead you will pass some ranch buildings on the right.

At 2.6 miles, ride over a mound, then through the white vehicle barriers and continue straight on the well-graded dirt road which begins climbing. After a long, mellow descent, pass Rainbow Ranch.

The road joins Highway 229/Creston Road at just over 5.7 miles. Turn around here and return the way you came. You will be back at the small mound and vehicle barriers at 8.9 miles. You will reach the top of the single track at 9.3 miles. Now enjoy the twisty single track descent. Cross the creek at 10 miles and continue on the dirt road, returning to the trailhead at 11.5 miles.

Rocky Canyon

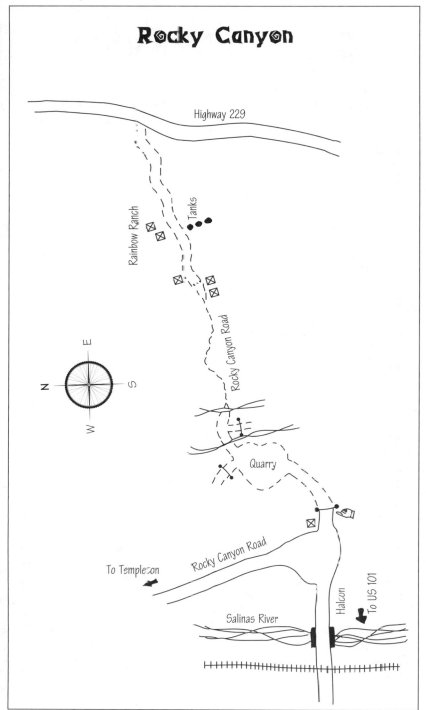

Highway 229

Rainbow Ranch

Tanks

Rocky Canyon Road

Quarry

Rocky Canyon Road

To Templeton

Salinas River

Halcon

To US 101

Cypress Mountain

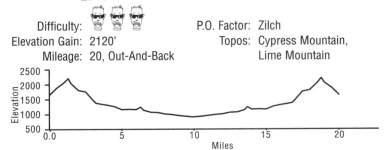

Difficulty: 😎 😎 😎   P.O. Factor: Zilch
Elevation Gain: 2120'   Topos: Cypress Mountain,
Mileage: 20, Out-And-Back   Lime Mountain

This is a long way up then a long way down. It's a great training ride for intermediate and advanced levels.

Getting There

From San Luis Obispo take US 101 heading north to Paso Robles. Exit at Highway
46 West and take it 10.5 miles to Santa Rosa Creek Road. Turn right and go just
over a mile to the intersection with Cypress Mountain Road. Park here. (If you live
in north county, you may want to do the ride in the opposite direction and park
near the Las Tablas County Fire Department on Chimney Rock Road.)

The Ride

Start climbing Cypress Mountain Road immediately. Just under the one-mile-
mark you will come to a wide spot in the road with lots of driveways. Stay on the
road as it continues climbing. Just ahead you'll start a much needed descent.

Follow the road as it descends toward a creek, passing a cement creek crossing at
3.3 miles. The road flattens and passes a campground at 4 miles. You will cross a
couple of wooden bridges before starting a gradual climb away from the creek.

At 6.3 miles you will pass a gated mining area and start your descent. You will
pass Klau Mine before coming to a fork at 6.6 miles. Go left staying on Cypress
Mountain Road. Just ahead cross a cement creek crossing and begin a series of
gradual climbs and descents.

You will pass several pens and corrals and a farm house at about 8 miles. The
road remains mostly flat as it cuts through pasture land until arriving at the Las
Tablas County Fire Department at about 10 miles. (Chimney Creek Road is just
ahead as the alternative starting point.)

Turn around here and head back the way you came. At the intersection with Klau
Road at 13.3 miles, go right remaining on Cypress Mountain Road. Climb to the
ridge top and enjoy a short descent before climbing again. You will pass the
campground at 16 miles and start the long climb to the ride's high point of 2110',
reached at 18.7 miles. Pass the wide spot in the road at 19 miles and descend
your last mile, 20 miles.

Cypress Mountain

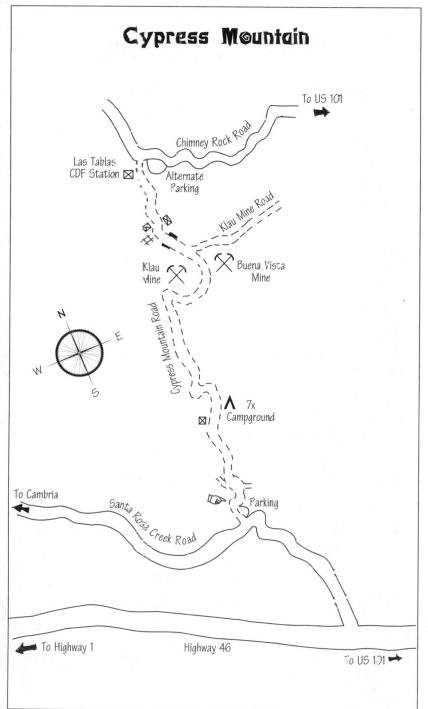

Kiler Canyon

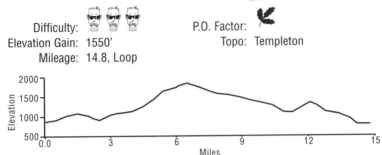

Difficulty: 😎😎😎   P.O. Factor: 🦇
Elevation Gain: 1550'   Topo: Templeton
Mileage: 14.8, Loop

Just outside of town, this scenic ride travels along a rarely-driven dirt road that winds through a tight canyon then climbs to a ridge top before a long, fast, paved descent.

Getting There
From San Luis Obispo take US 101 north to Paso Robles and exit at Spring Street. Take Spring Street to 1st Street. Turn left on South Vine, then right on Kiler Canyon Road and park on the street or in the dirt pullout just past the intersection on South Vine.

The Ride
Pedal up the paved road passing orchards on the right. It's fairly flat until 1.2 miles when a short climb begins. Pass Arbor Street at 2.2 miles and just ahead the road turns to dirt. After a creek crossing at 2.6 miles you will start another climb. At 3 miles two roads veer left, but stay to the right as the climb gets more gradual. At 3.5 miles you'll pass a sign marking the end of county maintained road. At 4 miles, the road narrows significantly and winds through a tight canyon. Just ahead, cross the creek and pass a road that cuts left. Keep going straight.

At 4.5 miles the road narrows even more and lots of poison oak encroaches on the sides of the canyon. You will start climbing out of the canyon at 4.6 miles. You'll come to a fork at 4.8 miles. Go right, continuing a long, steady climb. You will come to the top of the climb at 6 miles. Stay in the middle as the road forks to the right and left toward private residences, there is a cypress tree on the right. The road climbs, then descends until meeting Peachy Canyon Road at 7.1 miles.

Turn right onto paved Peachy Canyon Road heading downhill. After a series of curvy ups and downs you'll pass Old Settler Road on the right at 12.8 miles. Keep going on Peachy Canyon Road, reaching the Paso Robles city limits at 13.9 miles. Turn right on Olive Street at 14.3 miles. Just ahead, turn right on Vine Street. Pass 1st Street at the stop sign and return to the start of the ride reaching Kiler Canyon Road at 14.8 miles.

Kiler Canyon

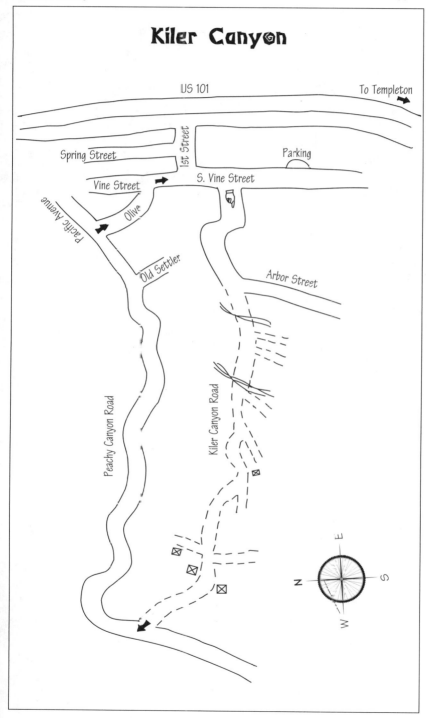

™

South County

South County Overview

Southern San Luis Obispo County offers a sampling of riding opportunities that simply can't be categorized. The area boasts a variety of landscapes, all well suited for mountain bikes. We have selected trails on the mountains, deserts and plains. No matter what your riding style, south county has something for you!

If you're looking for peaceful solitude, head to the Huasna area. This quiet valley is reminiscent of a simpler time. Nearby is the start of a vigorous ride from Lopez Lake, over the mountains and down into Pozo. This 29-mile ride is long, challenging and worth the effort if you're a strong rider.

Not too far away, off Highway 166, is another remote area with lots of trails. We've outlined a couple of rides in this area, but if you check a Santa Lucia Ranger District Off-Road Vehicle Map, you'll find quite a few trails that can be linked and combined.

The Carizzo Plain, located at the southernmost tip of the county, is a dream destination for geologists from around the world who travel there to study the seismic effects of the San Andreas Fault. The meeting place of the Pacific and North American Plates, the Fault runs along the base of the Temblor Range. While none of these trails directly cross the fault line, it can be clearly seen from several vistas.

Painted Rock is another highlight of the Plain. Once considered one of the most important remnants of Native American art in the United States, the large horseshoe-shaped rock stands as a monument to the area's early Chumash Indian community.

Nearby Soda Lake, a large natural sink, is a favorite destination for bird watchers. It is here that native prairie falcons and golden eagles are joined each winter by some 6,000 migrating sandhill cranes. In addition, wildlife enthusiasts may be able to catch a glimpse of the small herd of pronghorn antelope reintroduced to the plain.

While the area's characteristically hot and dry climate is not unusual to its natural inhabitants, visiting cyclists need to protect themselves with ample water and supplies. These trails are located in remote areas. Travel self-contained, as there are no services available near the trailheads.

South County Overview

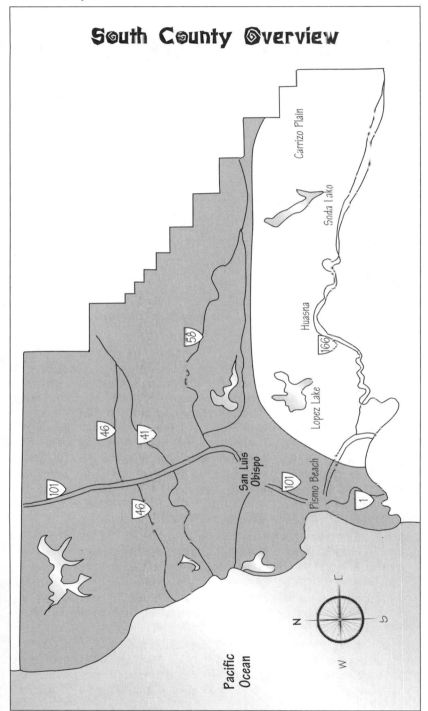

Carrizo Plain

Soda Lake

Huasna

Lopez Lake

San Luis Obispo

Pismo Beach

Pacific Ocean

Lopez Lake To Pozo

Difficulty: 😎 😎 😎 😎   P.O. Factor: Zilch
Elevation Gain: 3180'   Topos: Tar Spring Ridge, Caldwell
Mileage: 29, Out-And-Back   Mesa, Santa Margarita Lake

This beautiful back country ride crosses two mountain ridges and winds along creek beds on its way to Pozo. The round trip includes 24 stream crossings so expect to get wet during the rainy season!

Getting There

From San Luis Obispo take Orcutt Road to Lopez Drive and turn left. Continue on to Hi Mountain Road and turn right. Drive two miles to the Arroyo Grande Ranger Station and park there.

The Ride

Once on your bike, keep going on Hi Mountain Road passing ranches and homes on both sides of the road for the next four miles. Just after a steep climb begins, the road turns to dirt at 4.3 miles. It continues mostly uphill until 5.9 miles where it descends toward Salt Creek. Prepare for several creek crossings. Their first crossing is at 6.1 miles, the seventh at 7 miles. The road begins another steep climb. Cross another creek and continue climbing switchbacks away from Salt Creek.

At 8.4 miles you will reach the first high point, elevation 1880'. Take in the great views in all directions. At 9.7 miles you will cross Trout Creek. Just beyond is another stream crossing. The road then makes a long climb, reaching Hi Mountain Summit, elevation 2080' at 10.9 miles. (Garcia Ridge Trail is on the right.) From here, it's virtually all down hill to Pozo!

At 11.7 miles you will pass McNeil Spring and a sign marking the Los Padres National Forest boundary at 13 miles. Just beyond is another creek crossing and then you will cross the Salinas River at 13.6 miles. Just ahead, pass a gate and a farm house on the right.

You will arrive at the Pozo Ranger Station at 14.5 miles. If you're hungry or thirsty, the Pozo Saloon is just around the corner—serving great grub! (Open limited hours/days.)

Return the way you came, reaching Hi Mountain Summit at 18.1 miles. You'll descend all the way to Trout Creek reaching it at 19.3 miles. After a mile-long climb you will return to the first high point at 20.6 miles. From here switchbacks head downhill, reaching Salt Creek at 22 miles. Return to the Arroyo Grande Ranger Station 29 miles.

Lopez Lake to Pozo

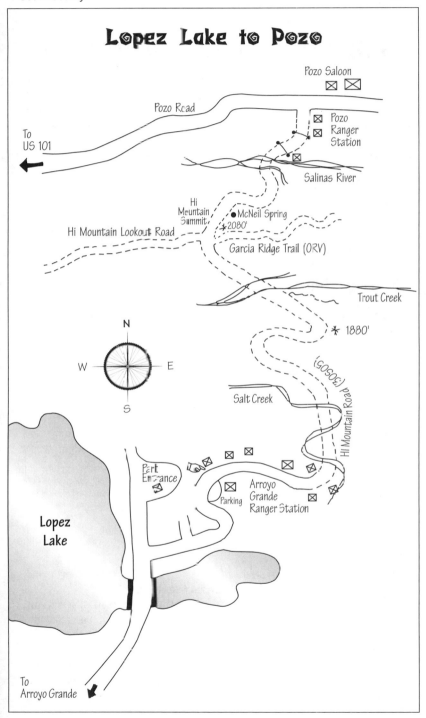

Pozo Saloon

Pozo Road

Pozo Ranger Station

To US 101

Salinas River

Hi Mountain Summit

McNeil Spring
2080'

Hi Mountain Lookout Road

Garcia Ridge Trail (ORV)

Trout Creek

N

W   E

S

1880'

Hi Mountain Road (30S06)

Salt Creek

Park Entrance

Parking

Arroyo Grande Ranger Station

Lopez Lake

To Arroyo Grande

Upper Lopez Canyon

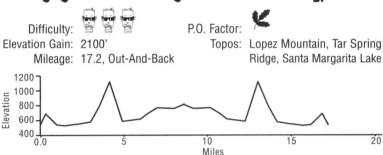

Difficulty: 😎😎😎   P.O. Factor: 🦶
Elevation Gain: 2100'   Topos: Lopez Mountain, Tar Spring
Mileage: 17.2, Out-And-Back   Ridge, Santa Margarita Lake

If you're afraid to get your feet wet, this ride's not for you. There are so many stream crossings (some quite deep), we lost count. The water is a wonderful relief in the summer and a great skill tester all year long.

Getting There

From San Luis Obispo take Orcutt Road to Lopez Drive and turn left. Enter the Lopez Lake Recreation Area and park in the day use area near the entrance. (To shorten your ride, park at the Equestrian Staging Area.)

The Ride

Once on your bike, keep going on Lopez Drive through the campground, past the water slide and swim areas. At 1.4 miles bypass a locked gate marked "Touoski Trail/High Ridge Trail." This dirt road is the start of the Wittenberg Trail. Just ahead, pass High Ridge Trail. At 2.1 miles, turn left at the fork going toward Touoski Trail.

After a creek crossing you will enter the grounds of Camp French. Turn right, leaving through the main gate and immediately turn left on the paved Upper Lopez Canyon Road. Now begin climbing.

After a steep climb and descent, bear right at the "Y" at 4.9 miles, staying on the paved road. Just ahead you will pass a conference center on the left and some Forest Service signs on the right. The road turns to dirt.

You will pass the Little Falls trailhead on the right at 6.4 miles. Keep climbing for about a half mile before descending. You'll pass the trailhead for Big Falls on the right at 8.5 miles.

Keep going until reaching a steel sign marking mileage to Lopez Canyon Trail, Sulphur Pots, Upper Lopez Canyon and East Cuesta Ridge Road. This is a good turnaround point. (The road does continue, but is not clearly marked and is completely washed out in many sections. If you decide to proceed, be prepared to ride/hike directly through the stream several times in search of the road.)

Pass the Little Falls trailhead at 10.8 miles. At 12.2 miles you'll pass the conference center and begin a big, long climb out of the canyon. You'll reach the top at 13 miles. Enjoy the long downhill, turning right into Camp French at 15 miles. Immediately go left on the dirt road and cross the creek. Turn right on Wittenberg Trail. You'll pass the locked gate at 15.7 miles and return to the start of the ride at 17.2 miles.

Upper Lopez Canyon

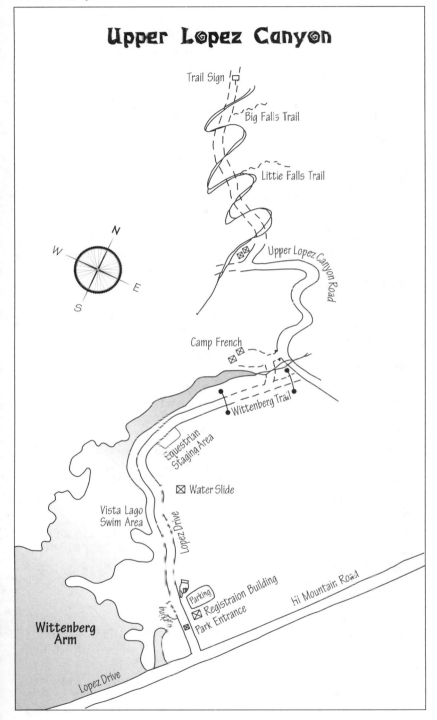

Trail Sign

Big Falls Trail

Little Falls Trail

Upper Lopez Canyon Road

N
W   E
S

Camp French

Wittenberg Trail

Equestrian
Staging Area

⊠ Water Slide

Vista Lago
Swim Area

Lopez Drive

Parking

⊠ Registration Building
Park Entrance

Hi Mountain Road

Wittenberg
Arm

Lopez Drive

Two Waters

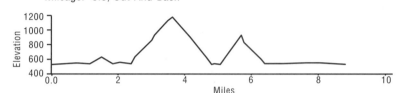

Difficulty: 😎 😎 😎   P.O. Factor: 🌿
Elevation Gain: 1290'   Topo: Tar Spring Ridge
Mileage: 8.8, Out-And-Back

This is a fun single track that runs along the north end of Lopez Lake. Well maintained and picturesque, with a couple of technical sections thrown in for a great ride.

Getting There

From San Luis Obispo take Orcutt Road to Lopez Drive and turn left. Continue on to the Lopez Lake Recreation Area entrance and pay the day use fee. Continue along Lopez Drive past the swimming and water slide areas and park near the Equestrian Staging Area.

The Ride

Pedal over to the trailhead at a steel gate, marked "High Ridge Trail, Touoski Trail." Just around the bend, pass the High Ridge trailhead. At 0.7 miles turn left at the "Y" following the sign toward Touoski Trail. Just ahead, cross a creek and enter Camp French. Keep to the far left and follow the trail signs.

You'll be at the start of Touoski Trail just under 1.2 miles. The lake is on the left. Take the single track. At about 1.5 miles you'll start a descent. At 1.8 miles pass a sign marking Two Waters and Camp French. You'll pass another trail sign at 2 miles.

At 2.4 miles bear right at the fork heading uphill on Two Waters Trail. (You'll see a poison oak sign.) The trail switchbacks up the hill.

You will reach the junction with Duna Vista Trail at 3.1 miles. Turn left going uphill. The vista point is reached at 3.6 miles, elevation 1178'. Enjoy the views.

Returning to the junction with Two Waters Trail, turn left heading downhill toward the Lopez Arm of the lake. As you approach the lake, notice a trail sign on the right as well as several forks.

A boat dock is at the left, the lake is straight and a pit toilet and the Ecinal Ecology Camp (permit camping area) is at the right. Ride down to the water's edge before heading back. At 5.7 miles you'll be back at the fork with Duna Vista Trail. Bear left, going downhill toward the Wittenberg Arm of the lake.

At 6.4 miles turn left at the "Y" onto Touoski Trail. At 7.6 miles, the single track ends at Camp French. At 8 miles turn right on the dirt road just before the main camp entrance. Cross the creek, and then turn right on "Wittenberg Trail." Keep going until arriving back at the trailhead at 8.8 miles.

Two Waters

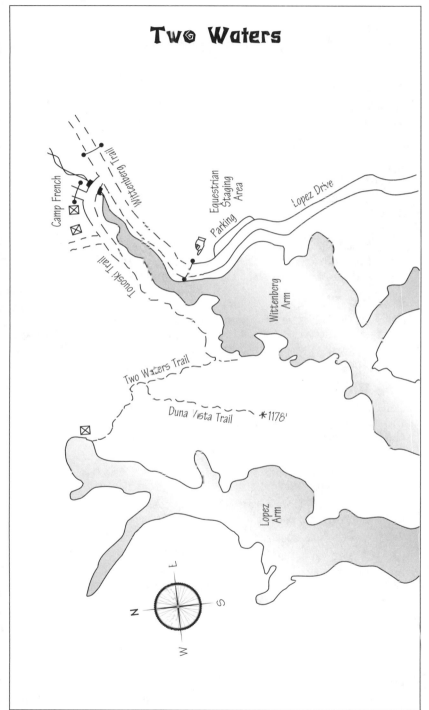

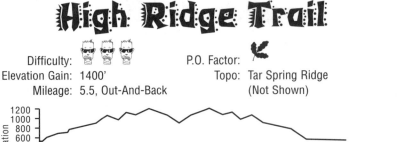

High Ridge Trail

Difficulty: 😎 😎 😎   P.O. Factor: 🦃

Elevation Gain: 1400'   Topo: Tar Spring Ridge
Mileage: 5.5, Out-And-Back   (Not Shown)

This is basically all steep ups and downs. If you don't like climbing, forget about it. But if you want to test your ability and crave steep, loose descents, you'll like this ride. There are also lots of short, unmarked side trails worth exploring.

Getting There

From San Luis Obispo take Orcutt Road to Lopez Drive and turn left. Continue on to the Lopez Lake Recreation Area entrance and pay the day use fee. Continue along Lopez Drive past the swimming and water slide areas and park near the Equestrian Staging Area.

The Ride

Starting at the steel gate marked "High Ridge Trail, Touoski Trail," pedal down Wittenberg Trail. Just around the bend, take High Ridge Trail as it climbs steeply. At 0.5 miles go right at the fork. Soon, the single track curves and another trail cuts in from the left. Ignore it and continue climbing.

You'll pass a big rock and reach the top of a climb at about 1 mile. Now descend. At 1.4 miles keep going straight as another trail cuts right. (A trail sign is on the left.)

At 1.6, elevation 1060', you'll have a clear view of the campground on the right. At the far left, you can see Pine Ridge, appropriately topped with pine trees.

You'll reach the top of another climb at 1.7 miles. You can see Lopez Lake on the right and Upper Lopez Canyon Road on the left near the trail. Keep going.

At 1.9 miles go left around the knob of the hill at the junction. Ahead at 2.3 miles, veer right at the fork near a trail sign. Now descending, you'll come to a fork with Blackberry Springs Trail at 2.5 miles. Just ahead, Turkey Ridge Trail splits off to the left. Both of these trails are off limits to bikes. This is a good place to rest before starting the tough climb out. (A horse trail continues straight up the hill following firebreaks.)

At 2.7 miles follow the trail sign straight. You'll pass a junction at 3 miles. Go right downhill. You'll pass another trail cutting left at 3.6. Keep going straight. Pass the big rock at 3.9 miles.

At 4.5 miles make a hard right at the fork heading downhill. You'll drop onto Wittenberg Trail at 4.8 miles. Turn left. You will return to the trailhead at 5.5 miles.

High Ridge Trail

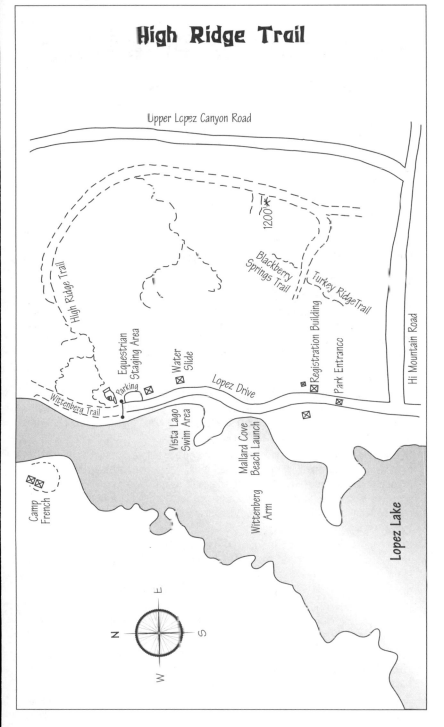

Huasna Rd. to Pine Ridge

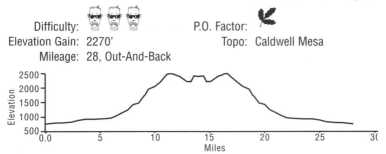

Difficulty: 😎 😎 😎   P.O. Factor: 🌿
Elevation Gain: 2270'   Topo: Caldwell Mesa
Mileage: 28, Out-And-Back

This ride meanders through the peaceful Huasna Valley to some interesting Chumash petroglyphs and an outstanding vista point from the edge of Pine Ridge.

Getting There

From San Luis Obispo take Highway 227 (Broad Street) south 12 miles to Huasna Road and turn left. About 2 miles ahead, turn right continuing on Huasna Road (Lopez Drive goes straight.) Follow the signs to the Huasna Area. Continue straight, passing the Huasna Townsite turnoff. You will reach the Huasna River bridge at 28 miles as the road turns to dirt. Park on the side of the road just before the bridge.

The Ride

Pedal across the old wooden bridge. Just ahead you will pass a ranch on the right. At 0.7 miles you will come to Forest Service signs noting private property lies on both sides of the road. Another sign notes a locked gate 10 miles ahead, passable only by hikers, bikers and equestrians. Keep going.

Over the next few miles you will cross four cattle guards before crossing a creek at 4.4 miles and another one just after. The road is fairly flat and an easy ride. You will encounter several more creek crossings and cattle guards before arriving at a fork at 9.1 miles. Turn left going toward Agua Escondido Campground and Stony Creek (right goes to Joughin Ranch/private property). Just ahead, pass through an open gate and then cross a cattle guard.

At 10.4 miles pass another cattle guard and a road cutting right. Keep going straight and start climbing. Just ahead, the road to Agua Escondido Campground drops down to the right. But keep going on the main road.

At 11.4 miles you will pass a parking area, some Forest Service signs and the road to the Avenales Observation Point. Keep going. At 11.7 miles you'll come to a steel gate. "No Trespassing" has been welded into the gate. This is public land and legal to proceed. Bypass the gate and keep going.

At 12.2 miles, go left at the fork. At about 13.2 miles you will come to 11 steel fence posts on the right side of the road. Directly across from these posts, take the single track going through the field. Cross the creek and go right at the fork just ahead.

As you start climbing, take either the single track or the double track. You will come to Garcia Potrero, a meadow surrounded by dramatic rock formations and trees. Follow

Huasna Road to Pine Ridge

the trail to an unusual rock formation. The trail splits around the rocks. Leave your bike and climb the rocks to find the Chumash petroglyphs. Be sure to sign the visitors' sheet on the east side of the rocks.

At the south end of the rocks follow the trail about .10 miles to the edge of Pine Ridge for fantastic views. Back on your bike, head back the way you came. You'll come to the road at 14.7 miles. Turn right. Take another right at the fork at 15.7 miles. You'll come to the locked gate at 16.2 miles. At 18.8 miles, go right at the fork and keep going until crossing the bridge and returning to your car at 28 miles.

Gifford Ranch

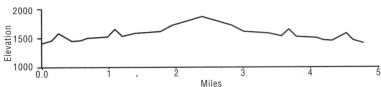

Difficulty: 😎 😎 😎   P.O. Factor: Zilch
Elevation Gain: 960'   Topo: Miranda Pine Mountain
Mileage: 4.8, Out-And-Back

Because of the steep climbs, we've limited the mileage on this little-known trail. But if you're ambitious, you can link it with ORV trails off of Highway 166. Consult your topos and a Santa Lucia Ranger District Off-Road Vehicle Map.

Getting There

From San Luis Obispo take US 101 south and exit at Highway 166. Travel east for 26.7 miles. Pull into an unmarked dirt drive on the left, passing through a barbwire gate. You can see some Forest Service signs near the parking area.

The Ride

Pedal out the single track located at the far left side of the barbwire fence. It soon passes an interesting rock formation on the left. Just past the rock, you will start a short, steep climb. Travel along a stream bed for a ways before climbing again. Just ahead, go right at the fork.

Start climbing on what is now double track. You will come to the top of the ridge at just under 0.3 miles. A transmission tower is on the left. Head downhill on the steep, rutted trail. You will come out at a cattle pond. Cross a creek bottom and pick up the single track straight ahead.

Pass through a barbwire gate at 0.6 miles. Follow the trail as it cuts between two large rocks and climbs the ridge. After a series of turns you will start climbing away from Highway 166.

Just under the 1-mile-mark you will make another steep climb. The trail soon plunges steeply through some rocky sections where you will have to walk your bike. At the bottom, turn left onto the double track.

After a couple of creek crossings, you'll pass a water trough on the left at 1.8 miles. Just ahead, you will start seeing debris, then corrals and cattle pens before arriving at the old Gifford Ranch house at 2.4 miles.

The house is in bad shape (what's left of it), but a nostalgic reminder of the area's past. Turn around here and head back the way you came. (If you want to keep going to connect with ORV trails, continue around the house and climb the ridge. Be sure to consult a map beforehand.)

Upon returning, you'll reach the top of the first climb at 3.7 miles, the barbwire gate at 4.2 miles and the top of the next ridge is just under 4.6 miles. Head downhill, returning to the trailhead at 4.8 miles.

Gifford Ranch

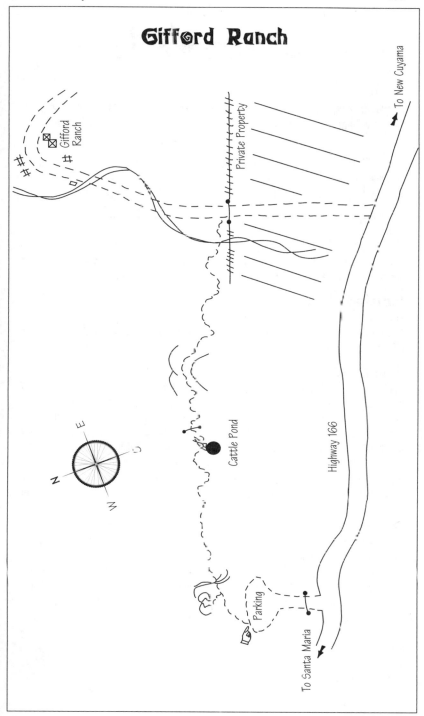

Adobe Trail

Difficulty: P.O. Factor:

Elevation Gain: 2840'

Mileage: 18.5, Loop

Topos: Chimney Canyon, Los Machos Hills, Branch Mountain, Miranda Pine Mountain

This is a tough ride and not suitable for neophytes. You'll get a workout and the chance to see the awesome "Big Rocks," huge rock formations.

Getting There

From San Luis Obispo take US 101 south and exit at Highway 166. Head east on 166 for 26 miles and turn left under an archway that says "Rock Front Ranch." Veer left following the road to some Forest Service signs. Park and start your ride here.

The Ride

Pedal back out to Highway 166 and turn right. Ride 4.1 miles, turning right into a gated parking area marked "Adobe Trail, Branch Creek, Thirty-Five Canyon." Take the single track through the gate at the end of the lot. (You'll be glad you warmed up on the highway as this single track immediately starts a long, steep climb.) Follow the switchbacks uphill. The dilapidated Permasse Adobe can be seen below as the trail clings to the steep hillside.

You'll reach the top of the climb at 5.1 miles. The trail soon descends into a creek bottom. After crossing the creek a couple of times you'll come to a water trough at 5.5 miles. Several creek crossings later, you will begin climbing out of the canyon.

The top of the ridge is reached at 6.1 miles. Turn left going uphill. Pass through a barbwire gate and continue climbing. At 6.6 miles the trail forks. Bear right on the well defined single track.

Follow it as it descends to a cattle pond at 6.9 miles. Ride across the earthern dam and pick up the single track near two oak trees. Take it as it gently climbs the ridge. At the top, turn right. A single track and a faint jeep trail run parallel. Take the jeep trail and continue as splits right going downhill between two trees.

Climb over a green steel gate at 7.5 miles and begin a short, steep climb. You are now on Twin Rocks ORV Road. At the "Y" bear right. (Shaw Ridge ORV Road goes left.) Just after a cattle pond, bear left at the fork on Logan Ridge ORV. At 9.4 miles turn right at the fork heading downhill. An overgrown firebreak cuts in at 10.3, but stay on the main road going downhill. You'll come out at a cattle pen at 11.2 miles. Turn right onto Branch Creek Road.

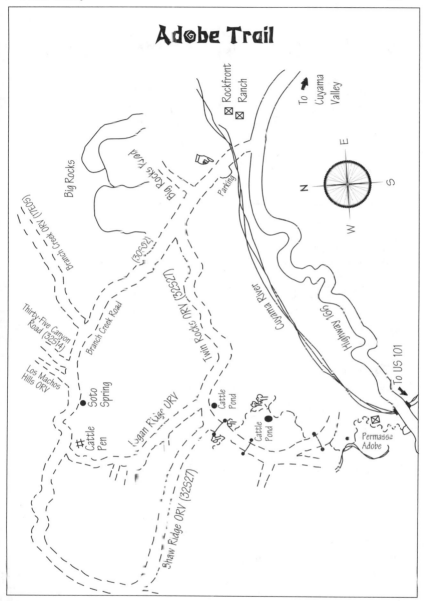

Adobe Trail

You will make lots of creek crossings over the next few miles. There is a small cattle pen on the right at 13.7 miles. Just ahead, pass Soto Spring. Machos Hills ORV Trail cuts left at 14.3 miles, but continue straight.

Entering the Big Rocks region at 15.9 miles, you will encounter a few more climbs and descents. The real steep sections are paved. At 16.2 miles bear right (Branch ORV goes left). Twin Rocks ORV cuts in from the right at 16.9 miles, but bear left and continue on to your car, 18.5 miles.

Caliente Mountain Trail

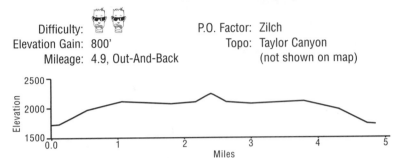

Difficulty: P.O. Factor: Zilch
Elevation Gain: 800'   Topo: Taylor Canyon
Mileage: 4.9, Out-And-Back   (not shown on map)

This is a fun, short single track that winds along the barren foothills of the Calientes. Overall it's fairly easy, but there are a couple of challenging climbs.

Getting There

From San Luis Obispo take US 101 south and exit at Highway 166. Travel east for 39 miles. On the left, a small "Public Access" sign and a pair of green steel access gates mark the trailhead. Park on the highway shoulder.

The Ride

Pass through the gate and close it behind you. The trail is easy to follow, as yellow and white carsonite easement markers have been placed approximately every 250 feet. You will soon pass some signs marked Caliente Mountain Trail. Continue climbing on the winding single track.

After several tight turns and passing through a small grove of pines, you will reach another gate at 1.9 miles. You can clearly see the Caliente Mountain Range straight ahead. Continue on.

You will come to the last easement trail marker at about 2.4 miles near two wooden posts. Ahead is a wilderness study area and off limits to bikes, so this is your turnaround point.

Turn around here and enjoy the fast, rugged descent. Return to the trailhead, 4.9 miles.

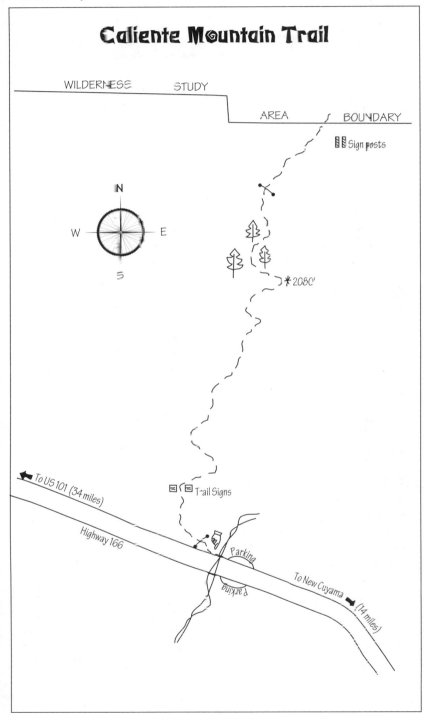

Caliente Mountain Trail

WILDERNESS   STUDY

AREA   BOUNDARY

⛰⛰ Sign posts

N

W   E

S

✳ 2080'

← To US 101 (34 miles)

⊡ ⊡ T-ail Signs

Highway 166

Parking

Parking

To New Cuyama ➤ (14 miles)

Soda Lake

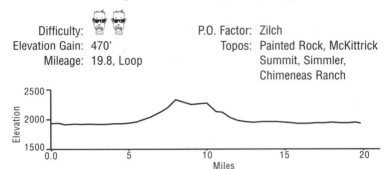

Difficulty: 👤 👤   P.O. Factor: Zilch
Elevation Gain: 470'   Topos: Painted Rock, McKittrick
Mileage: 19.8, Loop   Summit, Simmler,
                                                                    Chimeneas Ranch

Wildlife enthusiasts will love this easygoing ride. And the 6-mile side trip to Painted Rock, an ancient Chumash Indian ceremonial site, is quite interesting as well.

Getting There

From San Luis Obispo, take US 101 north to the Highway 58/Santa Margarita exit. Pass through town, crossing the railroad tracks. Drive another 45 miles to the Carrizo Plain and turn right on Soda Lake Road heading toward California Valley. Continue another 10.2 miles, turning right onto the dirt road for Soda Lake Overlook. Park in the lot. You may want to hike up to the top of the knoll for a great view of the valley.

The Ride

From the parking area turn left onto Soda Lake Road. At 2.2 miles turn right on Seven Mile Road. At 6.9 miles it turns to pavement at an intersection. Turn right on Belmont Trail. As you climb the slight incline, you can see Soda Lake to the right. Turn right on Elkhorn Road at 7.7 miles.

At 9.7 miles turn right on Simmler Soda Lake San Diego Creek Road. At 12 miles you'll pass a water tank and cattle pens. Continue on toward Soda Lake.

You will cross a cattle guard at 13.1 miles. Soda Lake is on the right. Stay on the road as it follows the contours of the lake, until reaching pavement at 15.4 miles. Just ahead, turn right onto Soda Lake Road. (For the 6-mile side trip to Painted Rock see below.*)

Continue on Soda Lake Road until reaching the Soda Lake Overlook turnoff, 19.8 miles.

*Turn left on Soda Lake Road, then turn right 0.8 miles ahead onto a dirt road. Turn left just past the Guy L. Goodwin Education Center. Follow the dirt road to the parking area 2.7 miles ahead. No bikes are permitted on the path to Painted Rock, so walk the short distance. Some ancient Chumash paintings still remain on the overhangings of this mysterious rock. (Periodically, Painted Rock is closed to self tours. Check in at the Education Center for a guided tour.)

Soda Lake

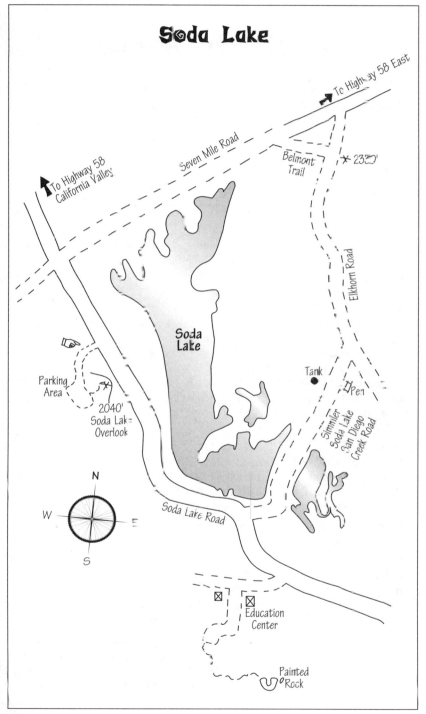

To Highway 58 East

To Highway 58
California Valley

Seven Mile Road

Belmont
Trail

2350'

Elkhorn Road

Soda
Lake

Parking
Area

2040'
Soda Lake
Overlook

Tank

Pen

Simmler
Soda Lake
San Diego
Creek Road

N

W   E

S

Soda Lake Road

Education
Center

Painted
Rock

Caliente Ridge

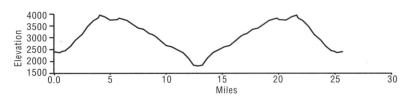

Difficulty: ☠ ☠ ☠ ☠
Elevation Gain: 4350'
Mileage: 25.7, Out-And-Back

P.O. Factor: Zilch
Topos: Painted Rock,
Caliente Mountain

This graded dirt road begins on the Carrizo Plain, climbs over the Caliente Mountains, then descends to the floor of the Cuyama Valley. This BLM road is subject to temporary closure due to inclement weather.

Getting There

From San Luis Obispo, take US 101 north to the Highway 58/Santa Margarita exit. Pass through town, crossing the railroad tracks. Take Highway 58 another 45 miles to the Carrizo Plain and turn right on Soda Lake Road. After passing Soda Lake, the road makes a sharp bend to the right as Simmler Soda Lake San Diego Creek Road joins from the left. Approximately 2 miles ahead, turn right onto a dirt road marked "Access to Public Land." Follow it 3.8 miles to Selby Cow Camp. Turn left and continue on about 1 mile to the Selby Parking Area.

The Ride

From the Selby Parking Area, pedal back up the dirt road to the fork. Turn left and begin the steep climb toward the Caliente Ridge Parking Area which is reached at the top of the climb, 4.1 miles. Once at the top, turn right. (The trailhead for Caliente Mountain, the highest point in San Luis Obispo County, is to the left but off limits to bikes.)

Various side roads cut in from all sides, but stay on the main road which is virtually all downhill for the next 9 miles. You will pass the FAA radio beacon at 5.8 miles. Great views await just around the corner.

At 8.7 miles you will come to a large intersection of many roads. Head straight through, passing a sign that says "Watch for Trucks." A side road cuts left at 12.4 miles, but continue straight. After a long downhill you will reach the canyon floor and a gate marking private property at about 12.8 miles.

Turn around and make the long climb up the ridge. You will reach the junction of several roads at 17 miles and the FAA beacon at 19.8 miles. The top of the climb is reached at 21.6 miles. Head downhill the way you came for a fast, fun ride down the mountain. At 24.9 miles turn right at the fork, reaching the Selby Parking area at 25.7 miles.

Caliente Ridge

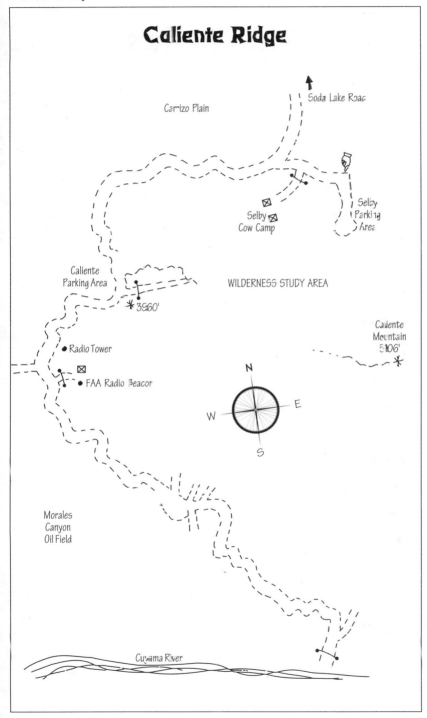

Soda Lake Road

Carrizo Plain

Selby
Cow Camp

Selby
Parking
Area

Caliente
Parking Area

WILDERNESS STUDY AREA

✳ 3960'

Caliente
Mountain
5106'
✳

● Radio Tower

● FAA Radio Beacon

N
W   E
S

Morales
Canyon
Oil Field

Cuyama River

Ride Index
(Alphabetical)

Ride Index
(By Difficulty)

Difficulty	Ride	miles	elevation gain	page
👤👤👤	Santa Rita Road	21.4	2060'	58
	Bl nn Ranch Trail	13.8	1820'	66
	Cold Canyon	9.6	610'	68
	Rinconada Trail	5.0	990'	72
	Hi Mountain Lookout Road	19.8	2360'	74
	Crazy 8s Loop	11.7	2040'	76
	Cypress Mountain	20.0	2120'	86
	K ler Canyon	14.8	1550'	88
	Upper Lopez Canyon	17.2	2100'	96
	Two Waters	8.8	1290'	98
	High Ridge Trail	5.5	1400'	10
	Huasna Road to Pine Ridge	28.0	2270'	102
	Gifford Ranch	4.8	960'	104
👤👤👤👤	West Cuesta Ridge	25.6	3850'	26
	Ferrandez Trail	18.6	2760'	78
	Lopez Lake to Pozo	29.0	3180'	94
	Adobe Trail	18.5	2840'	106
	Caliente Ridge	25.7	4350'	112
👤👤👤👤👤	West Cuesta Ridge Diehard V.	39.8	4570'	28
	Garcia Ridge	16.6	3300'	80
	Pine Mountain	31.6	3540'	82

Did you borrow this book?

If so, now is the time to order your very own copy!

Send the completed order form below and full payment to:
FAT TIRE FUN, Mail Order Department
P.O. Box 2000
Los Gatos, CA 95031-2000

For bulk purchases, call FAT TIRE FUN at (408) 395-4663

- - - - - - - - - - - - - - - - -

Please send me _____ **book(s) at $14.95 each.** $_____

I am including $3.00 for shipping and handling. $ 3.00
($3.00 shipping and handling fee is for up to 5 books per shipment.)

California residents add appropriate sales tax $_____
for your county of residence
                                          TOTAL $_____

☐ Enclosed is my check or money order, payable to FAT TIRE FUN.
   No cash, credit card or C.O.D. orders please

Ship to:

Name _____

Address _____

City _____ State_____ Zip _____

Phone (_____) _____ Fax (_____)_____

E-mail _____

Allow up to six weeks for delivery.

Gotta Suggestion?

Do you know of a trail not contained in *Fat Tire Fun* that should absolutely be here? Or do you have news of trail rerouting or closures? If so, we'd like to hear from you.

Remember, if you're making a new trail suggestion, the trail must be legally open to mountain bikes.

Mail to: FAT TIRE FUN
              P.O. Box 2000
              Los Gatos, CA 95031-2000

Or FAX: (408) 354-7095

Dear Gwen & Dirk:

The following is a:

❑ New Trail   ❑ Trail Rerouting   ❑ Trail Closure

My name is: _____

You can reach me at _____) _____

My address is _____

City_____ State_____ Zip Code _____

Fax: _____

e-mail: _____